THE CRUCIFIXION OF THE JEWS

THE CRUCIFIXION
OF THE JEWS

Franklin H. Littell

HARPER & ROW, PUBLISHERS

New York, Evanston, San Francisco, London

The author wishes to express his thanks to Temple University for a Faculty Research grant and to the Memorial Foundation for Jewish Culture for assistance during the period of this writing.

FIRST EDITION

Designed by Sidney Feinberg

Library of Congress Cataloging in Publication Data

Littell, Franklin Hamlin.
  The crucifixion of the Jews.

  Includes bibliographical references.
  1. Christianity and antisemitism. I. Title.
BM535.L53 1975   261.8'34'51924   74-32288
ISBN 0-06-065251-9

CONTENTS

Face loved of little children long ago,
　　Head hated of the priests and rulers then,
　　　If thou see this, or hear these hounds of thine
　　　Run ravening as the Gadarean swine,
Say, was not this thy Passion, to foreknow
　　In death's worst hour the works of Christian men?

—SWINBURNE
"On the Russian Persecution of the Jews"

INTRODUCTION

For centuries Christians have presumed to define *the old Israel, the Hebrews, the Jews, Judaism,* and so forth in ways generally patronizing, contemptuous, or demeaning. The habit began at the theological level among the gentile church fathers, was reinforced at law during the millennium and a half of "Christendom," and in the modern period has led directly to genocide. None of us who could have passed among the executioners during the Holocaust rather than being listed with the victims can escape the awful burden of blood guilt which that set of facts lays upon us. To the superficial mind, Antisemitism is simply another form of race prejudice, and only those are guilty who willfully indulge in it. Theologically speaking, however, the problem of sin and guilt is lodged much deeper than faulty intention or even corruption of the will. For a professing Christian, the red thread that ties a Justin Martyr or a Chrysostom to Auschwitz and Treblinka raises issues far more serious than can be dealt with by conscious avoidance of vulgar anti-Jewish slurs in speech or discrimination in practice. If we are, as we profess, linked in "the communion of saints" across the generations with those who have died in the faith, we are also linked in a solidarity of guilt with those who taught falsely and with those who drew the logical consequences of false teaching. That false teaching has led in our own time to mass rebellion of the baptized against the God of Abraham, Isaac, and Jacob, and to wholesale apostasy.

1

The cornerstone of Christian Antisemitism is the superseding or displacement myth, which already rings with the genocidal note. This is the myth that the mission of the Jewish people was finished with the coming of Jesus Christ, that "the old Israel" was written off with the appearance of "the new Israel." To teach that a people's mission in God's providence is finished, that they have been relegated to the limbo of history, has murderous implications which murderers will in time spell out. The murder of six million Jews by baptized Christians, from whom membership in good standing was not (and has not yet been) withdrawn, raises the most insistent question about the credibility of Christianity. The existence of a restored Israel, proof positive that the Jewish people is not annihilated, assimilated, or otherwise withering away, is substantial refutation of the traditional Christian myth about their end in the historic process. And this is precisely why Israel is a challenge, a crisis for much contemporary Christian theology.

Israel and the Holocaust are alpine events deeply resented by many modern Christian teachers—the former, because its survival against great odds requires a theological reappraisal for which few are ready; the latter, because popular religion admits error but denies guilt. Yet the crucifixion of the Jews is an unavoidable reality, and the avoidance of its implications for the churches is a shameless fact. As Gerald Strober's four-year study fully documents, the major Protestant publishing houses in America have simply swept the issue under the rug and turned their faces elsewhere—presumably to more salable and less painful messages.[1] The basic in-group problem is that the churches, whose leaders have been taught to think "scientifically" and "objectively" about all truths, and to relativize primordial events into meaningless abstractions, no longer know how to face issues like "crucifixion" and "resurrection." They are as helpless in such confrontations as they are in dealing with "sin" and "guilt."

No wonder then that a number of Jewish leaders, speaking more bluntly than the majority of rabbis of goodwill, have questioned whether continuing conversations with church leaders are worth the effort. For dialogue is not empty social conversation; it is a verbal encounter aimed at a deeper perception and appropriation of truth. Dialogue which does not lead to self-examination and self-correction is a foolish sham. If we who profess Christ do not, when push comes to shove, care whether Jews live or die, sooner or later it will be evident to the partner —even if not to ourselves—that our dialogue is but foolishness, our utterances but a tickling of the jaded ears.

The last self-justification of Christians is to demand that "the Jews" change. Almost admitting that we must change, and radically, we find diversion from our own guilt by pointing out the wrongs done by "the Jews." To speak in such language is, of course, itself but a thinly veiled expression of Antisemitism. But beyond that, it is a stance of bad faith. John the Baptist or Paul of Tarsus, who would have perished in a Death Camp, had the right to speak harshly to their fellow Jews. (But in no single word did either of them imply an end to God's covenant with Abraham and his seed!) An American gentile Christian, whose government was silently complicit in the Holocaust and whose cobelievers (whether Protestant, Orthodox, or Roman Catholic) shared in the operation of the camps, has no ground on which to stand validly to criticize "the Jews."

Perhaps the Jewish people and faith would be strengthened by appropriating truths from Christianity. If so, and if Christians correct their teaching and action sufficiently to make such an idea credible, the Jewish teachers will in due time say so. In the meantime our problem is the incredibility of Christianity. It is not the Jewish people that has become incredible; it is Christianity and those who call themselves "Christians." Therefore, so far as Christian thinkers are concerned, the words that hit like hammers and burn like fire (Jeremiah 23:29) must be addressed first and singly in this generation to our own condition; our task is not the condition of "the Jews," but the condition of "the Christians."

A book like this has one built-in problem. A basic affirmation is *the right of the Jewish people to self-identity and self-definition.* No sound dialogue, let alone friendship or brotherhood-love, can develop if one partner is constantly endeavoring to categorize, to define, to box-in the other party. That has been the malaise of Christianity's relation to "the Jews" for centuries, and it is only slightly healed if the old malice is purged and an open invitation issued to "the Jews" to assimilate. That has been the modern style of "friendliness"—among nationalists, liberals, Marxists. Martin Luther invited "the Jews" to convert, and when they did not, he became a virulent Antisemite. The children of the Enlightenment invite "the Jews" to assimilate, and when they do not, the Enlightened also regress to Antisemitism.

What is it if not presumption for us to assume that "the Jews," called by God to be carriers of history, should desire to blend into the gentile world? Here again the modern humanitarian line of thought is deceptive. For a "Christian" to pursue such doctrine is not only unjust to the Jewish people; it also reveals a fundamental flaw in the doctrine of the church, for the church —where it in truth exists—is also called to be a counterculture. *Gleichschaltung* (homogenization) should be as repugnant to believing Christians as it is to practicing Jews. If our modern, enlightened "Christians" were more certain of their own calling, they would have less difficulty in comprehending God's continuing call to the Jewish people.

Those comparatively few Christians who maintained their integrity during the Holocaust did in fact challenge the dominant culture, and some thousands perished. A good many more suffered persecution as a counterculture to totalitarian creeds and systems. But that does not excuse the rest of us, who wittingly or unwittingly accommodated; certainly it does not cover the apostasy of the millions who collaborated. The vast majority of those who suffered martyrdom as witnesses to the truth of God in the twentieth century were Jews.

The built-in problem is this: while affirming the right of the Jewish people to self-definition, the Christian must deal with the truth that he cannot achieve his own identity and self-definition apart from the role of the Jewish people in meaningful history. That meaningful history, as contrasted with our prebaptismal chronicles from the time when we were aliens, strangers, "having no hope, and without God in the world" (Ephesians 2:12), requires an affirmation of the positive role of

the Jewish people—yesterday and today. The displacement
myth, advanced by the gentile church fathers and repeated
without biblical justification ever since, solved the problem by
praising the dead Jews of the distant past (patriarchs, prophets,
and lawgivers) and teaching contempt for living Jews. A reconstructed and genuinely Christian theology will have to deal
affirmatively with the contribution of the Jews in the last two
millennia as well as with our fathers-in-God before the Christian era.

Rabbinic "Judaism"[2] found it possible to elaborate the historic mission of the Jewish people without special reference to
Christianity. The same truth of God, revealed before the Christian churches appeared, continued to be valid and binding.
Although Jewry cannot define itself without reference to the
gentiles, and here the biblical dialectic of chosenness and universalism comes into focus, the Christians simply count as gentiles. The Christians come under the Noachite laws in the same
way as other gentiles. Christians (and Muslims), however, cannot define themselves without reference to the Jewish people.
Both Christians and Muslims have traditionally disposed of the
problem by use of a displacement theory (see pp. 28f., 31). But
even a more just and brotherly statement of the relationship
cannot avoid the paradoxical truth that the Jews do not need
the Christians, as such, to understand their mission in history;
but the Christians need the Jewish people. The most difficult,
if not impossible, prospect for the Christian church would be to
have to live and work in a world without Jews. The Christians
need the Jewish people as a "model" of peoplehood in God's
work in history, and they need the living interaction with the
people of the Torah.

A definition of the relationship is essential, therefore, but it
must be fundamentally different from the falsehoods taught in
the past. What specific form the corrections must take can only
be aimed at, not precisely hit upon, at this time. The wrong is
too long-standing, and the immediate guilt is too great. At the
most important level, the hymns and prayers and songs and
readings of worshiping families and congregations must achieve
a new focus. The conceptualizations of the theologians will only

be valid and vital, in any case, to the degree that they are rooted in the faith of a believing Christian people. For this reason, two documents are appended to this book. The first, "A Statement to Our Fellow Christians," was prepared over a four-year period by a distinguished company of Roman Catholic, Protestant, and Orthodox theologians, for study in the churches (p. 134). The second, a Yom HaShoah liturgy, was prepared for the use of Christians who share with the Jewish people in memorial to the victims of the Holocaust (p. 141).

I am convinced that—with all the implications involved for theology and church history—the crucifixion and resurrection of the Jewish people are the most important events for Christian history in centuries. I hope that my handling of the discussion will be edifying to fellow-Christians and at least avoid offense to Jewish readers. The path we walk is like one strewn with buried land mines. I plan to explode as many as possible that were planted by Christians, and I count on the chairty of Jewish friends if I walk too clumsily on ground hallowed by Jewish blood.

NOTES

1. Gerald S. Strober, *Portrait of the Elder Brother: Jews and Judaism in Protestant Teaching Materials* (New York: NCCJ/AJC, 1972). The Strober study followed on the classic study of Bernhard E. Olson, *Faith and Prejudice* (New Haven: Yale University Press, 1963).

2. Like *Antisemitism, Judaism* is an unsatisfactory and finally misleading term. Both words became current following the Enlightenment, and they say either too much or too little. "Antisemitism" is a word created by the earliest anthropologists (ca.1780), who believed that since etymologists had created systems of "Semitic" and "Aryan" language-groupings (ca.1740) therefore there must be "Semites" and "Aryans." Enthusiasm for the rubric *Aryans* has waned since the Third Reich, but the daily newspapers still carry owlish letters informing us that "the Arabs" cannot be "anti-Semites" because they are "Semites" themselves. Since the word is here to stay, it should be used in its plain meaning: hatred of the Jews *(Judenhass)*, and it should be spelled without the hyphen. *Judaism* was a word made current by early professors of comparative religious studies, who found it useful to create some general "religious" categories. It was also much easier to discuss "Hinduism," "Buddhism," "Christianity," "Judaism," and so forth on a flat plane than to try to fathom the mysteries of any of them. (Such mysteries were "obscurantist," "superstitious," and "unscientific,"

anyway!) Kierkegaard advanced a telling brief that to treat Christian faith as a "religion" was to abort it. In any case, "Judaism" bogs down early as a tool of discussion; there is no "Judaism" or "Jewish faith" separate from the Jewish people.

Judaism is sometimes used for convenience in this book, as in this case, but the reader is warned against abstracting or spiritualizing the term. Docetism is still widely found among "Christians," although it is a heresy; among Jews, a split of the "spiritual" and "material" has no place at all. The case of the American Council on Judaism is symbolic: starting out with an eighteenth-century method of intellectual abstraction, it ended in Antisemitism (in one of its nastier forms: Jewish self-hate). Liberal Protestantism has often followed a parallel course, ending in *positives Christentum* (Article 24 of the Nazi Party Platform) or "civic religion."

I

THE LANGUAGE OF EVENTS

To master history and to come to some meaning of it requires far more than awareness of a multitude of facts. Since the ocean of facts is infinite, the imposition of some order on the inchoate mass of evidence immediately requires a process of selection. The choosing of what persons, events, and stories are to be emphasized as more important than others involves a selectivity which is inevitably to some degree personal and subjective. If his heart is in it, so that the narrative flows at times with passion, the element of the writer's personal commitment looms larger. But it is always there, even among those who fail to recognize their own finitude. The one who reports on his dialogue with the past/sense of responsibility in the present/vision of the future can only say: "This is the way it seems to me," and sign his name.

Since his view of history is intensely personal, a writer must be critically aware of his own fallibility. A model of such a candid statement of self-awareness can be found in the introduction to the seven-volume *History of the Expansion of Christianity* written by the great Christian historian Kenneth Scott Latourette.[1] In it the author introduces himself, his place in the religious scene, his critical training, in a way to help the reader understand by whom he is being guided as he studies the record. In an age when so many faceless persons are writing so much propaganda, a good deal of it anonymous and Antise-

mitic, the trained mind will be grateful for such candor. Before
semiliteracy was widespread, the world of writing and reading
was a small community; today the careful identification of
sources has become imperative.

The careful participant in the dialogue will ask himself, "Who
is talking?" "What are his credentials?" "Is a credible witness
speaking?" He will demand identification of others and will-
ingly give it himself. Consider the circumstances which have
thrown the American churches into the preliminary stages of a
church struggle in the last decade. The sources of attacks on the
Christian churches, many of whom make millions in the process, are often people who fall into the following categories: (1)
religious adventurers who use the titles *Reverend* and *Doctor*
though their degrees are traceable to diploma mills; (2) agitators from outside the country who claim to be authorities on
communism in the American churches; (3) low-level ex-military
types who team up with professional ex-Communists.

Of this intellectual and spiritual malaise, with results so evident in "Watergate" and related horrors, a wise judicial mind,
Louis Nizer, has aptly written: "Are such people to be trusted
when they turn a fanatical cheek the other way? Has their
character been reformed with their change in position? Having
once adopted the credo that lying is virtuous if it serves the
cause, this conviction may persist when the cause has changed.
. . . I have always doubted their reliability, no matter to which
side they gave their allegiance."[2] Do I wander? I think not.
Renegades from Jewry have played a considerable role in the
development of cultural Antisemitism. And apostates from the
churches have shaped the post-Christian ideologies and systems
which attack and/or undermine Christianity today. The second
most famous forgery in Western history—after the Donation of
Constantine, which Lorenzo Valla exposed in 1440—is *The
Protocols of the Elders of Zion.* And the *Protocols* were, after
the Koran, the most frequently cited book at the International
Conference of Muslim Scholars gathered in Cairo in 1968. According to recent report, King Faisal of Saudi Arabia is presenting a beautifully printed and bound copy of the *Protocols* to
each of his Western visitors. In Western Christendom the *Proto-*

cols are seldom sold or cited today, except by the Fascist underworld; in Muslim countries, largely prescientific in their world view if not their technology, the *Protocols* stand next to holy scripture. But lest we congratulate ourselves too unreservedly, let it be mentioned that when the killers came for the last of the Russian czars, in the revolution of 1917, they found on the bedside table of Nicholas II—the "little Father" of Russian Orthodoxy—two books of pious devotion: the Holy Bible and *The Protocols of the Elders of Zion.*

One of the basic contributions of science, of the historical method to the rules of the dialogue, is the awareness that sources must be checked carefully. The trained mind will check its sources, and it will also be aware of its own finitude. It will face honestly the truth that the choice of stories to be told, the identification of events to be emphasized, the periodization of historical eras and episodes, introduce a whole world view. How are certain events singled out as more crucial than others? On what basis do we affirm that the Exodus, Sinai, the return from the first exile, Golgotha, the destruction of the Temple, the Fall of Rome, the fall of Constantinople, the Reformation, the Enlightenment, the burning of Moscow, the Holocaust, a restored Israel, and a united Jerusalem—all or a selected portion of these formative events—are more important to our view of history than, say, the Battle of Waterloo or Custer's Last Stand?

The answer to such a question cannot be given lightly. Neither can it depend solely upon individual arbitrariness. For implicit in each is a general consensus, a shorthand of conversation, concerning meaning in history. To a considerable degree the identification of symbolic events defines the whole view of history, and while that has its subjective aspect, there is also an objective view of general history implied. It is important to keep in mind, therefore, that any writing about general history has its personal and subjective dimension and that the credibility of the witness is of fundamental importance; equally important is to distinguish what is really being said, what major truth is being conveyed, in the affirmation of certain events, certain periodizations, certain moments of crisis and decision in the historical process.

The View of History

When we turn our attention—with the assistance of identified participants in the dialogue—to the general view of history, we discover very early that there are involved not only critical appraisals but group memories. That is, the data of the past dimension of history include many unexamined stories and subconscious assumptions. Precisely at this point in the scientific discussion of "history" and of historical "facts" the understanding of the meaning of archetypal/formative/"epoch-making" events or "root experiences"[3] begins to loom large in importance.

The reason is clear. Every culture, and perhaps especially religious culture with its intensely personal dimension, relies heavily upon that which is memorized and repeated unto children and children's children. Indeed, a very high level of culture can be maintained upon the base of a vital oral tradition. More than that, the formation of sacred Scriptures has been profoundly influenced by the music, rhythm, and symmetry of generations of singers and storytellers—before the stories and songs and teachings were ever committed to writing at all.[4] But since the Enlightenment, since the transfer from the "hard sciences" to humanistic studies and even theology of what is loosely called "the scientific method," unexamined stories and subconscious assumptions have been in ill-repute. The emphasis has been placed upon hard "facts," preferably well documented.

Moreover, the process of generalization and abstraction, which—along with devotion to the mathematical model—is the genius of scientific progress, implicitly involves repudiation of the unexamined and mysterious. Most serious for our present purposes: it covertly carries the destruction of unique events and persons. There may have been a covenant with Abraham, but every tribe has had its ethnocentrism. There may have been an Exodus, but it is—according to "the laws of human society" —simply another example of the tendency of human tribes and families to wander across the face of the earth. There may have been a lawgiving at Sinai, but every tribe has had its lawgivers. There may have been a Golgotha, but Socrates drank the hemlock, Gandhi and Martin Luther King, Jr., were martyred, and after all this is a bad world for good men. There may have been a destruction and desecration of Jerusalem in 70 and 135 C.E., but Rome and Constantinople and Moscow and Dresden went through similar experiences. There may have been a Holocaust, but there is a large volume of other illustrations of "man's inhumanity to man." There may be a state of Israel (and this is less hypothetical to all but the most hardened), but there are at least half a hundred other new nations since World War II. In terms of the unique, the style of thinking moves from avoidance of the particular to generalization to abstraction to banality.

In short, the critical/analytical/comparative/abstractive method—unless balanced by aesthetic and/or religious awareness—can lead easily to absurdity in the treatment of the mysterious and the sacred. Contrary to the shallow mind, the Amish are not to be dismissed as "prescientific" because they fear the single-minded devotion to violence and *techne* which the dominant society values.[5] Neither are the Hasidim to be dismissed as "obscurantist" because they shy away from committing the central stories of the faith to paper.[6] Both are reacting to the unqualified hybris of an intellectual method, a human engine, which—unless carefully balanced by sensitivity to human finitude and fallibility—makes the profanation of the sacred a daily experience.

In a fine essay reprinted in Sister Katherine Hargrove's *The Star and the Cross*, Emil Fackenheim has exposed the limits of the inductive method in dealing with identity and life's central meanings. Prior to self-identity is awareness of the primordial relationship.

> A self is primordially open to other selves; and unless it were thus open it would never become a self at all. A child becomes an "I" in a relation of openness to a "thou"; indeed, he knows the meaning of "thou" before he knows the meaning of "I."
>
> . . . genuine love of God, which is openness to the Divine, can be known only in actual openness, and this is precisely what the critic

cannot and will not have. Hence he is left only with the images and feelings which are its by-product.[7]

To communicate to another person something which has been primordially experienced involves closure, but before closure there must be openness—or there will be nothing to relate.[8] The pursuit of wisdom requires openness; the communication of it requires closure. Most important for the present problem: just as the child is aware of the mother before it is self-aware, just as it commonly says mama before it says I, so the awareness of God and his work in history is primordially known to the person of faith. But the world of *techne*, in its aversion to the mysterious and open, has sealed off that dimension of human experience. From the elementary school, the young person is taught to think in the symmetry of the closed, the traditional mathematical model, and by the time he has finished with the university, he may be a skilled technician—but he is rarely a wise man.

Trained to abstraction, disciplined to work long hours with single-minded attention to one set of presuppositions and one idiom, conscious of membership in an elite technical fraternity that transcends national and cultural and religious boundaries, this technical expert is an interchangeable man. He can build bridges, guide missiles, or install pacemakers with equal competence for the Soviets, the Chilean junta, the Iraqi national socialists, or the Canadian federal republic. If he were a man of wisdom, he would be troubled in some alliances—or perhaps even impeded. But his training has oriented him to *techne* and denied him the *logos* dimension of knowledge. As for the meaning of God in human history, that dimension was excised long since—along with other unexamined and unexplained "data."

A schooled aversion to the mysterious, fortified by an abstract style of thinking that effects premature closure, has now produced several generations of "educated" men and women who are in truth but half-educated. And what they have mastered is the dangerous half at that, when wielded by persons without any fundamental commitments. The same kind of "educated" technicians built Auschwitz and the antipersonnel weapons used in Vietnam. The same kind of skilled technicians design the Russian legal artifices that justify sending dissenters to mental institutions and provide the American legal tricks that excuse breach of the Constitutional Bill of Rights by government agencies.

The technically competent barbarian is available to the highest bidder, be he communist or fascist or feudal despot or republican. The common mistake is to suppose this is solely a result of his avarice or unbridled ambition; it is aided and abetted by a system of education that has trained him to think in ways that eliminate questions of ultimate responsibility. Having eliminated God as an hypothesis, he exercises godlike powers with pride rather than with fear and trembling. Unaware of himself as a person, finite and imperfect, he becomes year by year less a mechanic and more a machine—a machine which is still able to perform some complex services that are yet beyond the capacity of even the most advanced computers.

Because the technological society has emerged so recently, because 95 percent of the scientists who have ever lived are alive today, because the big budgets of university research are almost all aimed at accomplishing specific technical results, the world of *techne* largely ignores the past in its devotion to present tasks. Thus its resolution of present problems is accomplished by a human interaction that neglects the dialogue with the past, and the problems themselves are defined by an intellectual discourse that rules out the mysterious and transcendent (except as that not yet laid conquest). That the definitions often lack aesthetic and spiritual quality and that the solutions are often morally outrageous—all this was programmed in from the start.

There are many—and essential—intellectual exercises that can only be carried on by bracketing out, for the time, major aspects of human existence. When the terms of a set of laboratory experiments are fixed, other experimental sets fall from the consciousness. When the time comes to report the results, closure is effected. So also with the application of the analytical/ critical/comparative method to the Scriptures: a certain method of intellectual discipline is rigorously applied; the data

are put on the rack that new insights may be extorted. But if
this is the only way of learning, the partial truths thereby gained
may obscure truths greater and more holistic.

If we use only the language of generalization and abstraction
and correlation, we may come to "laws of spiritual development" or "laws of human society" analogous to Kepler's "laws
of stellar motion" and Newton's "laws of gravitation." But the
"laws" once presumed to govern "hard science" have themselves been shaken by recent evidence. And in the areas of
social study and religion, where the reporter is protagonist as
well as subject, the approach was always of partial value. Finally, as Paul van Buren has well demonstrated in *The Edges of
Language,*[9] explanatory language gives out as we come to speak
of matters as heavily laden with mystery as, for example, "God"
and "love." The common vernacular works very well in a closed
report such as the description of a chair. An engineer with a
special competence and a peculiar idiom can round out a
finished description of a sophisticated machine. But as every
lover knows, to speak of love is not necessarily to love. Only the
person who loves, or is loved, knows love. Not seldom, when
closure occurs, love is gone. Perhaps more often than not, certainly in the gray and bloody twentieth century, the response
of the person of faith to the divine may well be silence: the
messenger is not sent, or very possibly he is terrified to report
the eclipse of God.

If, however, the university man is aesthetically and spiritually
incapacitated by miseducation, he will respond with the banali-
ties of abstraction. As a child of the Enlightenment, ignoring the
past and bracketing out the unique, he will effect closure and
utter a meaningless (and profane) generalization. Face to face
with the lawgiving at Sinai (Exodus 20:1 ff.), and particularly if
he is personally tempted to breach the law, he will recollect the
Code of Hammurabi, the Analects of Confucius, the mores of
the American Indians. Ten Commandments thus relativized
are less demanding. As Christians who collaborated with the
Nazis put it, the Jews had their customs, and we will have our
own Teutonic *Alttestament*—one confirmed by our own blood
and soil! Encountering what the Christians profess about the

event at Golgotha, we will take refuge in other illustrations or examples of heroic suffering and death, thus avoiding what such a unique event demands: either *yes* or *no!*

Turning to the Holocaust, the crucifixion of European Jewry (and the shocking possibility that this event may be the confirmation of the calling of the Jewish people to be the Suffering Servant), the child of enlightenment will still seek to escape by abstractions. Again and again we are reminded by letters, particularly from liberal Protestants, that not only the Jews were slaughtered in recent times: "Look what we did to the American Indians . . . Look what we did to the peoples of Vietnam." Even in cold-blooded logic, the response is a non sequitur. But what is really at work is the intellectual drive to find a generalization; for example, nations have often been cruel and bloodthirsty toward others. The hidden agenda is far more desperate: to find some means of escape, hopefully intellectually respectable, from the awful truth about the Holocaust.

One historian, lacking both aesthetic instinct and spiritual sensitivity, has referred to the Holocaust as another example of man's inhumanity to man. The bankruptcy of such banal utterance is transparent: the generalization is not even within the historical discipline; rather it is misuse of a once fine but now degraded phrase of moral philosophy. Intellectually, as well as spiritually, it is a shallow escape mechanism.[10] It is precisely as though a man, being caught in adultery, were to answer to his wife that sociological tables show such incidents to be rather common.

The way of thinking revealed is, if left to itself as exclusive master of the field, destructive of truth. It leads to vulgar profanation of the sacred. The messages of the covenant with Abraham, the Exodus, Sinai, Golgotha, the Holocaust, a restored Israel—to single out a few alpine events in the development of Christian faith—are unique. The story of each such event carries a mystery, a weight far beyond the literal and "factual." The important thing about a story is this: you either get it, or you don't. A listener may say yes or no to such a story, but if he seeks to avoid facing it by reversion to purportedly "scientific" generalizations, he shows intellectual and moral dishonesty.

The truth about the murder of European Jewry by baptized Christians is this: it raises in a most fundamental way the question of the credibility of Christianity. Was Jesus a false messiah? No one can be a true messiah whose followers feel compelled to torture and destroy other human persons who think differently. Is the Jewish people, after all and in spite of two millennia of Christian calumny, the true Suffering Servant promised in Isaiah?

The Story

The analytical essay evokes debate. Set in the tentative mood, it elicits hypothetical responses. The story evokes a total response. Recognizing himself in the situation described, or remembering a scene which has been part of his consciousness from earliest years, the listener responds with his whole self.

Most stories, however much the genius of an individual storyteller may embellish them, have been told and retold for generations. The tale of Robinson Crusoe is a good example. The castaway who comes to a mature philosophy of life that later confounds the schoolmen, primarily by communing with Nature and Nature's God, has been for centuries a favorite symbol for those who suspect sophistication, artifice, and the corruptions of civilization. The tale entered the English language in a 1642 translation from the Spanish, sponsored by two Quaker gentlemen of London. Back of the Spanish form, its origins have been traced through the Arabic of the Iberian peninsula to the Tale of Hayy—known to the Muslim storytellers of Damascus and Baghdad in the ninth century.[11] From that time and region the story vanishes into dim antiquity; some have found its traces in the legends surrounding the appearance of Alexander the Great upon the world scene. In each age, the story evokes the individual and group memory of a lost innocence, of a time and place with fewer complications and compromises, with less alienation from the world of true being.

Highly complex cultures can be supported by careful attention to the oral tradition. Among some peoples, young boys with musical ears and quick memorization capacity are set aside as living "libraries"—functioning for life as the persons to whom others turn when they need to have recalled the lessons learned by fathers and fathers' fathers. In the sacred writings of Jewish, Christian, and Muslim religions there are clearly discernible ancient stories that were repeated for centuries before being committed to writing. Criticism and analysis came much later. And in all three religions (as well as in many other cultures), memorization and dramatic recollection and reenactment have been basic to maintaining the vitality and integrity of the communities.

Missiologists tell us that it commonly takes three generations before the basic stories and central liturgical responses become part of the unconscious life of a converted tribe or extended family. Once such a musical foundation has been laid, critical and analytical and comparative study can begin. But if there is no primordial foundation, if there are no archetypal persons and events, or if the heritage has been destroyed by political or economic adjustments (or by common neglect), the scientific enterprises become self-destructive to the individual and to the group. The alienated man becomes disoriented and dehumanized as his cultural matrix fragments and withers away. Unfortunately, while it takes at least three generations to build up a rudimentary oral tradition, that foundation can be destroyed in one generation. With the overwhelming triumph of the technological in our schools, that is precisely what has happened in the last three decades in America. The method of thinking that is technologically produced has been pressed down to the fourth grade, and by the time the young people reach college and graduate school, they are frequently incapable of understanding idioms that carry other dimensions of learning.

Our schools teach social studies in the fourth grade, but the young emerge having never learned the Declaration of Independence, the Bill of Rights, the Gettysburg Address. Averse to memorization (except in mathematics and chemistry), the schools send the pupils forward without the psalms, without Shakespeare, without foreign languages, without music. They are thus deprived for life, for the time to memorize with ease is the years during youth and through puberty; after sexual maturity and the crisis of self-identity, the mind handles analysis and critique quite naturally but—unless continually disciplined by repetition and recollection—finds memorization increasingly difficult.

The experience with foreign languages is symbolic. The time to learn a foreign language is from the third through the tenth grade. Nothing is more painful to university teaching at graduate level than to watch students try to learn foreign languages at twenty-three to thirty years of age. The situation with musical culture is analogous. If a singing culture is maintained for generations, the people sing from early childhood through old age. If singing is neglected in schools and families for just one generation, tone deafness begins to appear in children, and in church an overly loud organ replaces the shattered fragments of congregational singing. With the evisceration of the oral tradition our schools are now successfully producing generations of young citizens who are musically, linguistically, and morally tone-deaf. These are technology's last and final products, programmed to self-destruct: the gravediggers of civilization and culture, the technically competent barbarians.

First the public school administrators pressed consolidation, massing the youth in overly large buildings with expanding problems of violence, taking the schools away from any influence by other youth-educating agencies—the family, the church or synagogue, the youth clubs. Then they established a curriculum and a host of administrative regulations which enforced the technological emphasis and starved the wisdom dimension. Then they established a closed shop, excluding from the teaching staffs the best-educated persons in the society and enforcing excessive methods requirements upon those who "went into education." Finally, the educational political machines commenced to starve out and harass those private schools where residual communities of counterculture (Amish, Mennonite, Seventh-Day Adventist, sometimes Roman Catholic or Orthodox Jewish) tried to maintain an oral tradition and resist the domination of a mindless technology.

The process of destroying the recollection and reenactment of the wisdom of the past has been aided, it must be admitted, by many of the denominations and church publishing houses.

They too have depreciated memorization and storytelling and stressed analysis. Symbolic is the decline in use of the King James Version (AV) in the liturgies. For the specialist and critical student there are, of course, more accurate and clearer translations. For the genuinely critical Christian scholar there are the Greek and Hebrew Testaments. A profound disservice has been rendered, too, by various "conservative" cliques who have tried to prove the King James Version to be more accurate scientifically. They have missed the point as badly as those "liberal" churches which hastened to plunge laymen and children into the maelstrom of critical and analytical (and necessarily skeptical) study.

The irreplaceable value of the Authorized Version was that it was supremely musical, had been a major force in shaping the English language in its purest style, and could be memorized and recited by congregational and family groups. Today we have constituencies that have learned just enough "science" to know that there are many translations, each imperfect in its own way; and they can neither tell the stories themselves nor join in congregational recitations. An oral tradition which for many generations sustained a religious culture, upon which to be sure critical studies could operate among exegetes and other scientists of religion, is well on its way to extinction.

The story, the report of a formative event polished by generations of memorization and narration, the music and rhythm and cadence of the record of God's work in human history—all are ignored in the common schools and treated frivolously by many of the denominational publishing houses. Enlightenment has triumphed and, with its triumph, brought darkness of the soul and dimness of vision.

There are still surviving some countercultures in which both *logos* and *techne* are given full measure of their worth to personal and community maturation. One of the special values of Jewish community life is the fact that, especially since the threat of extinction in the Holocaust and the renewal of life in a restored Israel, serious attention is given to both dimensions of knowledge. Here again the Jewish people is a "model" from which earnest Christians can learn. In Israel, about which one of the ruder untruths is the charge that the people are "secular-minded," one is continually aroused to admiration by the constant but perfectly natural evocation of biblical persons and events in daily conversation. And in America, a Christian who has had the privilege of participating in a Seder service can only marvel at the tenacity with which the Jewish family has maintained the beauty and truth of the language of events—and wish that his own church had a similar awareness of the truth that to have faith is to remember.

Why is it that so much of white Christendom is so impoverished in its oral tradition? (Here, it must be said frankly, the black churches and the Evangelical denominations are less damaged.) There are many explanations: the abandonment of a position of counterculture, along with consequent casual acceptance of the spirit of the age; assimilation into ethnic and racial and national cultures, with neglect of the separation scripturally enjoined; the surrender of discipline and integrity of religious community life to please the princes and powers of this world's darkness; the acceptance of social and economic status in return for neglect of the prophetic and discordant; the death of preaching and decline of corporate worship. Most of all, and here the church leaders are especially guilty, our spiritual crisis is the legitimate fruit of long devotion to a way of thinking which carries a partial truth, but which by itself and unchecked by a vital oral tradition has impoverished our language and our responses to the stories that confront us with our true identity.

Having destroyed history by neglect of memorization and recollection, having weakened even serious study by neglect of the biblical languages, having allowed spiritual and moral tone deafness to grow like cancer, we fancy ourselves justified as "Enlightened" men and women. We are in fact simply impoverished and rootless, "like a wave of the sea driven with the wind and tossed" (James 1:6). Every fad that comes along in the currents of the general society is seized upon, for a short session stressed as proof of the church's "relevance," and then quickly dropped as a more brightly flashing lure enters the stream of consciousness.

By contrast, the stories which make up the core of a living oral tradition guide the person to self-awareness, help him to place himself and his people in a wise understanding and response to the encounters which demand of him an answer. To give a personal illustration: for several years a colleague from the field of political science and I have taught an undergraduate course on "Genocide, Politics, and Religion." The Holocaust is the "model" by which we seek to test other homicidal governmental policies—in Vietnam, East Pakistan (now Bangladesh), Namibia, and so forth. In one session we were discussing the Exodus as an archetypal event, and several "Enlightened" students responded negatively: the Exodus was long ago and far away; the conscientious citizen should concentrate upon contemporary issues, like racial justice and peace. At this point there stood up in the class of eighty-two a black woman student, about ten years older than the class average, and she delivered a ten-minute impassioned statement on the importance of the Exodus. It soon became evident that she was talking about two events, one seen in the light of the other: the classical Exodus of the slaves from Egypt, and the exodus of her own family and people from slavery in the United States just a little more than a century ago. She understood her personal history by reference to one of the formative events of her religion. Her statement was in effect a faith affirmation, and by it she placed herself in history and securely established her own identity.

Without the language of events, she would have been as rudderless a bark on the sea of heterogeneous human events as her younger contemporaries. With the experience of black religion, which has so far done much better than most of the white churches in maintaining the vigor of the Christian oral tradition, she could respond with wisdom to a life question.

NOTES

1. Kenneth Scott Latourette, *A History of the Expansion of Christianity, I: The First Five Centuries* (New York & London: Harper & Bros., 1937), p. xvii.

2. Louis Nizer, *The Implosion Conspiracy* (Greenwich, Conn.: Fawcett Publ., 1974), pp. 204–5, on the credibility of renegades.

3. Emil L. Fackenheim, *God's Presence in History: Jewish Affirmations and Philosophical Reflections* (New York: Harper & Row, 1972), passim.

4. On the Christian experience, see Birger Gerhardsson, *Memory and Manuscript* (Uppsala: Almqvist & Wiksells, 1961), especially on the style of learning in the education of Jesus and the Twelve, and in the early church, pp. 12 f.

5. See my discussion of the Amish view of education in "Sectarian Protestantism and the Pursuit of Wisdom: Must Technological Objectives Prevail?" *Public Controls for Nonpublic Schools*, ed. Donald Erickson (Chicago: University of Chicago Press, 1969), pp. 61–82; also, "The Anabaptist Heritage and Oral Tradition," in *Report of the Conference on Child Socialization*, ed. John A. Hostetler (Washington, D.C.: HEW, 1969), pp. 253–64.

6. See Elie Wiesel's discussions of this issue in the introduction to *Legends of Our Time* (New York: Avon Books, 1970); and in *Souls on Fire* (New York: Random House, 1972), p. 64.

7. Emil Fackenheim, "On the Eclipse of God," in *The Star and the Cross*, ed. Katherine T. Hargrove (Milwaukee: Bruce Publ. Co., 1966), pp. 236–37.

8. Cf. Ray L. Hart, *Unfinished Man and the Imagination* (New York: Herder & Herder, 1970), esp. the concluding discussion of "the hermeneutical spiral."

9. Paul van Buren, *The Edges of Language* (Philadelphia: Fortress Press, 1973).

10. Henry Friedlander has thoroughly reviewed the various devices used by most contemporary historians to avoid facing the issue of the Holocaust; cf. "Publications on the Holocaust," in *The German Church Struggle and the Holocaust*, ed. Franklin H. Littell and Hubert G. Locke (Detroit: Wayne State University Press, 1974).

11. Antonio Pastor, *The Idea of Robinson Crusoe* (Watford, Herts.: Gongora Press, 1930).

II

CHRISTIAN ANTISEMITISM

Free-church men and other advocates of religious liberty have long held that when Christians ceased to be a nonresistant and persecuted remnant and became prosperous persecutors, the nature of Christianity was fundamentally altered. Often a "Fall of the Church" has been dated by the union of church and state under Emperor Constantine, or perhaps by the enforcement of approved doctrine under the same Augustus.[1] But those Christian writers who have noted the radical change between the teaching and style of life of early Christianity and the way of Christendom have seldom noted that it was accompanied by a radical worsening of the lot of the Jewish people. The time of Christian establishment was also the season when drastic decrees were passed in synods and councils against the Jews.

At the same time, Christian thought departed its Hebrew origins and embraced the speculative structures of pagan philosophy. There will be no attempt here to argue the question whether the New Testament is necessarily Antisemitic, an issue which is increasingly exercising the skills of exegetes. One thing is clear: the earliest Christians were Jews, and, however harshly a Jew may criticize his own people, his stance is vastly different from that of a gentile using the same proof texts and interpretations. Jesus and Paul and Peter would have perished at Auschwitz, a fact that latter-day gentile Christians dare not forget.

Occasionally, particularly in the modern period, deracinated Jewish intellectuals—children of the Enlightenment—have adopted concepts and used language which originated among gentile cultural Antisemites. But the only real Antisemitism among Jews is self-hate, a pathological condition among marginal Jews which has declined markedly with the rebirth of Israel.

Theological Antisemitism begins with the transfer of the base of the early church from Jewish membership to a large gentile majority. This happened fairly quickly. Paul's mission to the gentiles opened the way to a wholesale harvest of the thousands of gentile fellow travelers who attended the synagogues of the Diaspora. Scattered throughout the Mediterranean basin, these "God-fearers" flooded into the young Christian churches when the evangelists explained to them that the longed-for Redeemer had come and that in him men of all tribes and tongues might become true servants of the true God.

The family quarrel between the Christians and the majority of the Jewish people was intense enough when Jews who were Christian believers were wrestling with Essenes, Pharisees, Sadducees, Zealots, and other factions for the soul of the Jewish nation. But a man such as Paul, for all of his harsh language toward those who rejected the Christ, never in a single line implied God's rejection of the Jewish people. On the contrary, through faith in Jesus Christ the believing gentiles were grafted into Jewish holy history: "thou bearest not the root, but the root thee" (Romans 11:18). Previously the gentiles had walked in darkness—

> . . . without Christ, being aliens from the commonwealth of Israel, and strangers from the covenants of promise, having no hope, and without God in the world: But now in Christ Jesus ye who sometimes were far off are made nigh by the blood of Christ. For he is our peace, who hath made both one, and hath broken down the middle wall of partition between us (Ephesians 2:12–14).

Theological Antisemitism began with the gentile converts of many tribes, with their natural resentment of the priority of Israel, their resistance to the authority of events in Jewish his-

26   *The Crucifixion of the Jews*

tory, their pride in their own ethnic values, languages, cultures.

By the time of *The Teaching of the Twelve Apostles* (Didache, early second century), ill feelings toward "the hypocrites"—the Jews, professors of a false religion—are clearly evident (chap. 8). The scheduled feasts of the Jewish week fall on the second and fifth days; therefore, the Christians should fast on different days, Wednesday and Friday. Whereas early Jewish Christians had observed both the traditional Sabbath and the "Lord's Day," the first day of the week, the anniversary of Christ's resurrection, the gentile Christians' program began to delete the Sabbath.

In the *Epistles* of Ignatius of Antioch (ca.70–107), the de-Judaizing force of gentile Christian prejudice is also pronounced. Against a faction in the Christian churches that kept the Sabbath, Ignatius insists that only the "Lord's Day" is to be kept; Christians should make a point of *not* observing the Jewish Sabbath. In Ignatius' thinking the church is "the new Israel," the prophets and heroes of Israel were spiritual ancestors of the church and therefore "Christians before their time" and not properly part of the Jewish religion *(To the Magnesians)*. "We love the prophets also . . . having faith they were saved in the unity of Jesus Christ" *(To the Philadelphians)*. By expropriating the chief teachers and events of Jewish history, and by shifting the weekly calendar of the pious servants of God, the gentile Christians were thoroughly launched in that "de-Judaizing" process which has been the bane of Christianity. Thereafter, any Christian who taught the tradition and cultivated the customs of the early church stood out as a singular friend of the Jews, surrounded by gentiles who had deliberately cultivated distance from them. Soon the annual calendar of the Christians would cut Easter loose from its "model," the Passover celebration. A little later a new periodization of history would be elaborated, one which further alienated Christianity from the continuing worship and vitality of the Jewish people.

The Epistle of Barnabas probably dates from the first century, and until the fourth century it was included among the sacred books read out loud in Christian congregations. The writer was evidently an early gentile Christian, and he used the allegorical method of interpreting Scripture—the method taught in Alexandria and based on the Platonic doctrine of ideas. The Jewish Scriptures—selected portions of which were later to be designated "the Old Testament" in the Christian canon—were accorded respect through an allegorical exegesis which brings out the Christian and "spiritual" meanings but suppresses the historical and literal. Thus the uniqueness of events in specifically Jewish history is sacrificed. The author does not go as far as later gentile heretics like Marcion and most Gnostics, who cut the church from her Jewish heritage and denied the particularism and "materialism" of the Jewish Scriptures altogether, but it is evident that the connection made him nervous. A gentile, thinking like a Greek, he can appreciate Abraham's intended sacrifice of Isaac as "a type of Christ," but the plain historical sense of the story eludes him. In the end, the church takes the place of the Jewish people, and the writer denies that "the Old Covenant" was ever really in force.

The Epistle to Diognetus (ca.150) takes a jaundiced view of the Jewish faith and rarely cites the Jewish Scriptures to prove the case for Christianity. Chapter 4 is full of anti-Jewish feeling and expression, with explicit repudiation of Jewish ceremonial customs and conspicuous failure to use even the common line of Christian apologetic which appropriated the Jewish heritage even while referring negatively to the living Jews.

Altogether, theological Antisemitism is well advanced in the Apostolic Fathers (gentiles).[2] In the later church fathers, it takes a finished form—finished enough to justify the harsh imperial decrees of the Christian Roman Empire against "the Jews." By the time of Cyprian (d. 258), theological Antisemitism had reached the polished form which prevailed throughout succeeding centuries. His style of thinking can be found in almost all of the major church fathers, although Chrysostom is perhaps the most vicious of all in his diatribes against the Jews. In his *Three Books of Testimonies Against the Jews,* Cyprian wrote:

> There is a new dispensation and a New Law, with abrogation of the Law of Moses and the old temple (*15);
> The Man of Righteousness was put to death by the Jews (*14); they fastened Him to the cross (*20);
> Now the peoplehood of the Jews has been cancelled; the destruc-

tion of Jerusalem was a judgment upon them (*6); the gentiles rather
than the Jews will inherit the Kingdom (*23);

Finally, "by this alone the Jews could obtain pardon of their sins,
if they wash away the blood of Christ slain in His baptism, and,
passing over into the Church, should obey His precepts." (*24)[3]

Added to the ill spirit of the family quarrel which developed
early is now a posture of obsequiousness toward the Roman
authorities, of transfer to "the Jews" of guilt which was
primarily Roman. Truth was sacrificed to diplomacy.

By this time the deicide calumny is boldly asserted, nor has
it rested to the present day. Dorothy Day of *The Catholic
Worker* tells the story of how her friend Mike Gold, who became one of America's leading Communists, was tormented in
his boyhood by "Christian" street gangs as a "Christ-killer." It
is a tale often duplicated in a Christendom which for centuries
taught contempt for the Jews and transferred to the Jewish
counterculture its own guilt feelings from accommodation and
servility to worldly power and pomp.

In czarist Russia the top political leadership used the deicide
excuse to cover the pogroms, and the pogroms to divert attention from the real causes of popular misery. When a compas-
sionate Russian officer wrote a critical report on the sufferings
of the Jews in the pogroms, the czar—an ignorant and superstitious little man, to be sure—scratched a marginal note: "But we
must never forget that the Jews sacrificed our saviour and shed
his precious blood."[4] And Monsignor John Oesterreicher has
given us a detailed account of the extraordinary political pressure applied by Arab League governments and their "Christian" Antisemitic allies to prevent Vatican II from striking the
deicide calumny from the table of Roman Catholic teaching.[5]

The Displacement Theory

Gentile Christian Antisemites expropriated the Old Testament, to read back into it their own interpretations of the historical process, when they did not excise the Jewish component
altogether. And to the New Testament they applied the allegorical method to make selected texts convey a condemna-

tion of the Jewish people which the original wordings will not sustain. Jesus, in contending with other teachers for the soul of the Jewish nation, made exclusive claims. Some Jews accepted and followed him; the large majority of his listeners did not. Since the largest percentage of Jews was already living in the Diaspora (well before the destruction of the Temple in 70 C.E.!), most of the Jews of that time had never heard of Jesus. Theological Antisemitism was a gentile construct, false to the facts and grounded in violence to the Scriptures.

Paul, in struggling with the problem of how to graft believing gentiles into an essentially Jewish history of salvation, solved his primary problem with considerable skill. Warning against the presumption of those who challenge God's "arbitrary" choice of the Jews to carry history (Romans 8:14, 20), he affirms that the covenant with Israel still stands (Romans 11:1–2a) and explains how the gentiles who believe in Christ are grafted into salvation (Romans 11:11 f.). And in the end "all Israel shall be saved" (Romans 11:26), both faithful Jews and believing gentiles. In the other major New Testament writing which struggles with the problem of gentile salvation, Ephesians 2, the writer portrays the desolate state of the gentiles before they came through Christ to share in the promises to the Jews and celebrates the breaking down of the wall of partition between Jews and gentile Christians. That Paul believed in the final triumph of Jesus Christ cannot be questioned. That he taught the rejection of the Jewish people cannot truthfully be asserted.

Upon the deicide lie, based upon an Antisemitic distortion of the record of Jesus' trial and condemnation, many of the church fathers went on to indulge in a "high-minded" boasting of precisely the kind that Paul warned them against. And now, in truth, we have come upon the time when a theology of boasting triumphalism, which culminated in Christendom's murder of European Jewry, may have resulted in the fulfillment of the warning Paul gave against those who supplant gratitude with price of place: "take heed lest he also spare not thee" (Romans 11:21). That God is today in eclipse in Christendom, the sensitive perceive. The possibility that he may have turned utterly away from the rebellious and apostate Christians cannot lightly be dismissed. Who of Christendom can today say with calm certainty that, after what has transpired, he has not taken the kingdom from us and given it to others bearing fruits more worthy of repentence (Matthew 21:43, Luke 3:8)? Is he not able of the very stones to raise up children unto Abraham? And how can we be certain, after the gentile record of rebellion and disobedience, and after the Jewish record of crucifixion and resurrection, that these "new" children of Abraham are not in truth the very children of Abraham "after the flesh"?

If such thoughts are troubling to those who hear the Word speak of a righteous God, they do not disturb those who have written into the texts their own opinions, those who have corrupted Christianity and made it a closed circle of Antisemitic ideology. The genocidal note is already present in the superseding or displacement myths. If Hitler was a true son of Innocent III and Harun al-Rashid in requiring Jews to wear a special badge in public, the Nazi "final solution" was a logical extension of the thought of those church fathers and councils who declared God was finished with the Jewish people.

The superseding myth has two foci: (1) God is finished with the Jews; (2) the "new Israel" (the Christian church) takes the place of the Jewish people as carrier of history. The third step comes naturally to the gentile tribes when they go over into apostasy: to expunge the Jewish component altogether.

To construct a theological Antisemitism, it has been necessary to wrench the proof texts and to write into them something not there. Take two texts typically used as foundation for a displacement theory: the parable of the fig tree (Matthew 21:18–22) and the parable of the marriage feast (Matthew 22:1–10). The first tale, which is used to demonstrate Jesus' power over nature and the power offered the disciples in faith and prayer, has been adapted repeatedly by ideologues of displacement. The fig tree is said to represent the Jews. Jesus' malediction, "Let no fruit grow on thee henceforward for ever," is said to be fulfilled in the barrenness of later Jewry. But later Jewry was not spiritually barren, and this wrenching of the texts reveals far more about the spiritual condition of those who do it than it tells of those upon whom they shovel contempt.

The second tale, which is told to demonstrate the bounty of the giver to those who share in the feast, the importance of joy in the event, and the selectivity of participation, has also been turned against the Jews. They are said to be those first invited, those whose place has been taken by latecomers when the original guests fail to come in. Again, the story has to be twisted and allegorized to make it convey such a message, and such distortion comes not from faithful listening to the Word but from doing violence to it. True "hearers of the Word" listen carefully; they do not do all the talking, and neither do they project their own prejudices into it.

The superseding myth is not only highly speculative; in the course of things it has become a two-edged sword. For in succeeding centuries many new prophets and founders of religions have appeared, claiming their own teachings to supersede Christianity. One of these was Muhammad, who claimed to teach a truth that displaces both Jewry and Christianity. When Muhammad, a gentile, utters harsh denunciations of "the Jews," his status is like that of a gentile Christian teacher—essentially different from Matthew or John in use of the phrase "the Jews." And the Koran is in language and in function more harsh than the New Testament toward "the Jews," though not more harsh than the decrees of Theodosius or the Synod of Elvira. In Muslim teaching, "the Jews" are cast aside by Allah because of their disobedience (Koran 2:88, 4:46, 52, 5:13, 60, 64, 78), and they will be punished by hell-fire (59:3). Muslim community *(Umma)* is the best that has ever existed among men, and if the Jews and Christians had also believed (that is, on Muhammad and the Koran), things would have gone much better for them (3:110). Muhammad assumed for himself the Jewish expectation of a coming messiah (Deuteronomy 18:18), and he proclaimed himself the last and culminating prophet ("the seal of the prophets," 33:40).[6]

In the modern period we have several other displacements and supercessions, including Cao-Dai, Baha'i, and Marxism. Quite evidently, the superseding or displacement theory has built-in limitations. Most important of all: Jewry has not withered away and disappeared. Quite the contrary: while Christendom staggers and stumbles (Isaiah 51:22–23) and wobbles from fad to fad, the Jewish people is undergoing its greatest awakening and renewal in many centuries.

Modern Antisemitism

For the men of the Enlightenment, the solution to "the Jewish question" was the disappearance of the Jews through assimilation. The Jewish faith, redundant through its mysteries and particularisms, should evaporate in an enlightened modern age. Having rejected the mystery and the supernatural view of the Christian church as a separate people, a counterculture, they especially resented and resisted any idea of a Jewish community with its own historical mission and integrity. Many leaders of the Enlightenment, such as Hegel and Voltaire, were vehement and voluble Antisemites; others, like Kant, created structures of being, within which the Jewish people (and a faithful Christian church!) had no continuing place. As Judd Teller conclusively demonstrated in an important little book, *Scapegoat of Revolution,*[7] the Jews have had an increasingly difficult time under modern nationalism, liberalism, and socialism in maintaining their integrity and self-identity.

So far as the Jewish people is concerned, what links Stalin's nationality policy with Hitler's "nonsectarian religion," and the two of them with Arnold J. Toynbee's "history" and Charles Clayton Morrison's "Americanism" is the bitter and unyielding determination to prevent the Jews from being Jews.

It is true that Antisemitism is still evident in some "Christian" circles.[8] It is also true that some minor Fundamentalist groups have continued to assert an intellectual triumphalism that was once very common in Christendom:

> We want to say most emphatically that when Christ died on Calvary, the old Mosaic order died, never to be revived. . . . Judaism is a thing of the past. It is a glorious memory despite its limitations and its failings. . . . It may seem harsh to say that "God is through with the Jews" . . . nothing has been taken from the Jews as individuals. . . . But the fact of the matter is that He is through with them as a unified national group. . . . The Old Testament was the time of the

Jews. The New Testament era is the time of the Gentiles. . . . The
Christian Church is the legitimate heir and successor of Old Testament Israel.[9]

At first blush, this looks like a simple dehydrated statement of
the displacement myth. The revealing phrase is, however, this:
"Nothing has been taken from the Jews as individuals." This
formula does not derive from ancient teachers and synods of
the church; it is precisely the dogma of the Enlightenment.
"Everything to the Jew as an individual; nothing to the Jews as
a people." Here too is another interesting example of how the
propositions of the Fundamentalists, like the abstractions of the
"liberals," frequently derive from nonbiblical sources.

In point of fact, Evangelicals in America are generally more
dependable friends of Israel than liberal Protestants. Some of
the reasons are ideological, as a brilliant young Israeli scholar,
Yona Malachy, has shown in a book to be published (posthu-
mously).[10] There are two major influences that work among
"conservative" Protestants for a provisional friendliness toward
Israel. Out of Pietism, and in connection with the rise of modern missions, many devout Protestants have identified among
the signs of the closing of the age (a) the return of the Jews to
their homeland, and (b) the conversion of the Jews to Christ.
Out of Dispensationalism, which arose with John Nelson Darby
in England and was spread widely in America by Charles I.
Scofield, came the division of sacred history into definitive periods ending in the restoration of the Jewish hegemony. In the
penultimate period, Israel shall be reestablished on earth and
conquer the rulers of the heathen nations, while the Christian
remnant is gathered into heaven in holy rapture. Neither Pietism nor Dispensationalism allows self-definition to the Jewish
people; both represent a friendship which is provisional. But in
a world where the Jewish people has few friends, and Israel is
constantly victimized by the combined blocs of the Communists and the Arab League and their hangers-on, even such
tentative friendship has value.

Among liberal Protestants the picture is more ambiguous and
varied, but dependably darker. For many years Reinhold Nie-

buhr was almost the only leading theologian in America to see clearly the meaning of the Church Struggle—the struggle of a Christian minority in Germany against Nazi abuses—and the critical importance of the developing attack on the Jews. He was also almost alone in perceiving the need for a redefinition of the relationship of the Christian church to the Jewish people.[11] Of the more common type, Arnold J. Toynbee, with his reference to the Jews as "a Semitic fossil,"[12] is a good example. An Anglican gentleman of the nineteenth century, in earlier years active in the emerging ecumenical movement, Toynbee remained hostile to any sign that the Jewish people were effectively maintaining a viable counterculture. "Semitic fossil" is a conceptualization pseudoscientific in form, Antisemitic in content, and inaccurate in fact. His hostility to Israel was a predictable outcome of his resentment that the Jews would not stay fossilized, as the grand scheme of Toynbee history required. Toynbee, with his twenty-six thousand possible cycles of the rise and fall of civilizations, remained a pagan Greek in his view of history and a gentile ethnic in his resentment of the Jewish dialectic of particularism and universalism. Another example, thoroughly documented and reviewed by Hertzel Fishman, has been the editorial policy of such liberal church journals as the *Christian Century* and *Christianity and Crisis*. In recent years the *Christian Century* has grown more charitable, but during the critical years of nazism and the destruction of European Jewry, its editor was a consistent opponent of measures that would have saved Jewish lives, and he even opposed informing Americans of the facts of the unfolding tragedy.[13]

Christianity and Crisis, founded by Reinhold Niebuhr as a corrective to the *Century*'s flight from history into timeless truths and moralisms, has in recent years featured reports hostile to Israel and in its editorial policy has appeared to be against those Christians sympathetic to Israel's cause. Among other consequences, Professor Ursula Niebuhr—widow of the great theologian—asked that his name be removed from the masthead of the magazine. The importance of Israel to post-Auschwitz Christians was one of Reinhold Niebuhr's strongest convictions.

Liberal Protestant Antisemitism

The Antisemitism of liberal Protestants was analyzed in depth in Bernhard Olson's brilliant study, *Faith and Prejudice,* which is still the best study of the religious roots of prejudice although unfortunately overshadowed by the Glock and Stark series. In his study of the curricula of four religious groupings, Dr. Olson—later interreligious director of the National Conference of Christians and Jews—discovered that the most "liberal" curriculum was also the most Antisemitic. It was Antisemitic for the same reason it was also anti-Catholic and anti-Fundamentalist; that is, it was marked by a "predisposition toward abstraction" which rejected particularity and repudiated the peculiar history of any religious community.

The parallel to the German experience is striking. In Nazi Germany, the very center of Protestant Antisemitism was this type of "liberal" Christianity, for the Jews remained the irreduceable sign of a divinely ordered counterculture after the baptized gentiles had apostatized and become good Teutonic heathen again. Religion-in-general was heartily affirmed in the Nazi Party Platform from 1920 on: "The Party, as such, stands for positive Christianity, but does not bind itself in the matter of creed to any particular confession. It combats the Jewish spirit of materialism within and without . . ." "Positive Christianity" *(positives Christentum)* is the same thing in its thought structure as "nonsectarian religion," "spiritual religion," "civic religion"; it is religion-in-general, without intellectual discipline or ethical content beyond that imposed by the society at large. Professor Cajus Fabricius of the University of Berlin, personally a Pietist and professionally a liberal, gave the specifics of such a Christianity of accommodation:

> Every singling out of individuals, every separation of interests, confusion of opinions, every irregular appearance of selfish interests, everything that calls forth and emphasizes differences between individuals and between various groups is repellent to the spirit of National Socialism, since it disturbs the unity of the *Volk,* breaks up the team spirit and menaces the powerful solidarity of the nation.[14]

If the Christians had remained Christian, they too would have maintained a counterculture resting on higher ground than Teutonic *Volksgemeinschaft.* Some few in fact did, and were victims of the Nazi drive toward homogenization *(Gleichschaltung).* But most accommodated, leaving the Jews exposed as the sign of discordant and unassimilated thinking and life-style.

Such liberalism, whether in Germany or America or elsewhere, is uncertain in its confessions of faith and promiscuous in church membership. The lines of the baptized blur into the patterns and values of the dominant society: "There are no obligations imposed on members toward their own group which are not also considered obligations toward members of other groups."[15] That is, there is no sense of special vocation, of unique calling: Christianity becomes, not the commitment of a peculiar people, but rather *a* thin veneer over the real and controlling ethnic or national thrust. And the nation is blended into religion-in-general, into a final false universalism, by virtue of its messianic mission. Thus the "spirituality" and "nonsectarian religion" which began in resentment of the earthiness of human history, of the finitude of all human experience, of the particularism of all discreet events, ends in the most demonic political manifestation of all: the ideologically justified, modern, totalitarian state.

Dr. Olson went on to point out the final incoherence of those who oppose the dream world of "humanity" to all particularities: "All history is particular—the history of *my* group, *my* church, *my* nation. Unshareable symbols, ideas, customs, and observances arise within these specific histories."[16]

Emancipated thought, whether liberal Protestant or Marxist or other, has always had difficulty with the Old Testament and the Jews. The baptized gentiles ("Christians") can generally be counted upon to accommodate or apostatize provided the seduction or coercion is strong enough. The Jews, whatever their individual beliefs, then remain as the irritating reminder that God is God and man is finite, limited, short-lived, and that man's most furious visions and triumphant rages are but fleeting episodes in the scale of eternity. The specter of Marcion, that enlightened layman of old who published a Christian Bible purged of all Jewishness, is not yet laid. It haunts the pages of the second edition of *Die Religion in Geschichte und Gegenwart,* inspired the pamphlets of the *Deutsche Christen* during the Third Reich, and yet hovers over the printing presses of our church publishing houses that are so fearful of mentioning specific events like the Holocaust and a restored Israel.

The slide into the abyss began with enlightened affirmation of "spirituality," "humanity," "universalism": the language of speculation replaced the language of events. Professor André Lacocque of Chicago Theological Seminary has written of the finicky taste of those Christians of the post-Enlightenment period who have sought timeless truths and high spirituality and wished to divorce themselves from the paradoxes and concreteness ("materialism") of the Old Testament:

> Within such a perspective, it was not without frowning that pious and moral Christians read the records of men too "human" for their taste. Jacob the liar, Moses the murderer, David the adulterer, Solomon the idolatrous, the wars waged by Israel are not the most edifying models for readers looking for comforting ethical narratives. Besides, "Church" and state are so mixed up here, the concept of God's intervention in human history so desperately materialistic, and the people's feeling of being elected and chosen so particularistic, that it is really hard to "spiritualize" this Jewish book in order to match it with a truly Christian religiosity.[17]

Much of the attack on "secularity" and "secularization" in the churches, and the broad assault on "secularism" since the Quaker Rufus Jones introduced the theme at the Jerusalem ecumenical conference in 1928, derives from a fundamental disregard of the Old Testament and misreading of the basic message of the New.

Of course not only liberal Protestants have fled from history and the God of history. Professor Y. Harkabi of Hebrew University has shown in his recent study, *Arab Attitudes to Israel,* how a Sunni rationalist of modern type also rejects the Jewish people in the name of (false) universalism:

> Judaism is not a monotheistic religion but a tribal creed. . . . The "God of Israel" . . . is obsessed with his people, with the nethermost

details of their daily chores. He watches their daily obscenities and their sins without moving a hair. After a few pretentious overtures in the first pages of Genesis, he has spent all his time, energy and intelligence, while the rest of the cosmos rotted, to dispossess a wretched little people of their land, put them to the sword and enter "his people" into possession of land and whatever tree, beast or child who escaped his "wrath." The truth is that this god has never travelled, has never seen the world, not to speak of making it. He is a "country" man whose world ended with his tribe, beyond which everything and everybody is equally foreign and equally an enemy. In short, he is a regional, tribal, separatist god, with whom monotheism has absolutely nothing to do.[18]

Comment is unnecessary.

Neither can Marxism, with its false universalism, handle the truth carried by the Jewish counterculture. Who can forget Yakov A. Malik's tirade at the United Nations Assembly on October 21, 1973? "Fascism and Zionism are racist creeds. The Zionists have come forward with the theory of the chosen people, an absurd ideology. . . . That is religious racism." Of course Malik, the U.S.S.R. ambassador, was trying to divert attention from Russian complicity in planning and equipping the Yom Kippur attack on Israel, and almost any interesting lie would have served the same purpose. But the theoretical aspect of "operation rewrite" is significant. Malik had evidently suppressed the fact that Lenin taught the Communist party to be chosen in precisely that sense, the party and its "professional revolutionaries" being the carriers of history. And he had also suppressed the historical fact that the doctrine of divine election anteceded Zionism by three millennia. What is then the difference between the claim that the People of the Covenant is chosen to carry history and the assertion that the Communist party carries history? Just this: one is true, and the other is false. The latter is an artificial construct of recent vintage, basically a bastardization of a biblical truth, while the election of the Jews to serve God's purposes in holy history is a landmark event in both faith and history.

The rage for universal truths, accompanied by abandonment of holy events and the Scriptures that record them, came to dominate university thinking following the Enlightenment. It is this style of thinking that is the most fertile single source of liberal Antisemitism—whether religious or secular. This conceptualization cannot handle the truth of unique events, and neither can it manage the biblical dialectic of particularism and universalism.

Religion in Life, a liberal Methodist journal, has recently published an attack on Jewish particularism. The Jews of biblical event are portrayed as conspirators, saboteurs, subversives, a fifth column in Egypt and Babylon. Charging the Jews with the same offense in the modern period, the author judges: "It is not surprising that Hitler retaliated against the chosen race by decreeing that it was not the Jewish but the Arian [sic!] race that was chosen."[19] Obviously in the writer's judgment the Jews should have assimilated in captivity; the Bible is wrong in presenting their revolt against slavery and oppression as obedience to God. One hardly knows whether to be more offended by the liberal professor's attempt to reverse the message of the Word, by the ignorance of a supposed scholar who doesn't know the difference between *Arians* and *Aryans,* or by the editorial policy of a supposedly Christian journal in publishing such Antisemitic claptrap! This must be said in the writer's favor: he attacks the early Christians for the same perverse devotion to the covenant. He would have a hard time showing, however, that this has been a major Christian fault in the modern period. Blending into the dominant culture, accommodating to the spirit of the times, has virtually become the major enthusiasm of Christian political and social establishments.

A final example: in a book called *The Crime of Christendom: The Theological Sources of Anti-Semitism,* a liberal churchman manages eleven reasonable chapters. And then in the twelfth, called "The Jewish Dilemma," he demands that American Jews give up their existence as Jews: "assimilation or segregation, religion or nationalism, humanism or tribalism, in short, Judaism or Israel?" He praises the spirituality of the American Council for Judaism and concludes that "ethnic and cultural Anti-Semitism . . . was originally provoked and continuously nourished by the orthodox Jewish dogma of uniqueness." The

writer is obviously unaware that "the orthodox . . . dogma of
uniqueness" is also a Christian claim in those times and places
where Christians have been aware of their calling. He is also
ignorant of the fact that charging the source of Antisemitism to
Jewish particularism has been one of the major Antisemitic
ploys for many centuries.

With typically enlightened fervor the writer comes to his
conclusion:

> Is God a tribal deity or a universal reality? Is he interested in
> revealing himself only at a certain point in time, at a certain place,
> through a certain man, to a certain people?
>
> Only a cosmic universal faith can raise man above the particula-
> risms of the cult.
>
> The Spirit of the Space Age may help men to grow up metaphysi-
> cally, to abandon our ethnocentric and geocentric theology and to
> substitute a spiritual religion for a physical one.[20]

There we have it again: a "spiritual" religion without a fixed
place in history!

To the believing Jew or Christian this surge of enlightened
spirituality does not have the appeal of unique, remembered,
and relived Event. And if he thinks too, he will have some
misgivings about "the Spirit of the Space Age." He will think of
six million who died in scientifically designed Death Camps. He
will remember three million lovely and simple little Viet-
namese slaughtered by ruthless machines controlled by men
who think in abstractions. There is a line connecting Auschwitz
and Mylai, but it is not discerned in abstractions; it is defined by
the truth that a "Christian" civilization's attitude to Jewish history and treatment of the Jewish people afford the litmus test
as to how it will act on all critical decisions involving the resistance of helpless or weaker peoples.

The mission of God's elect is to represent the coming final
triumph of justice and righteousness, mercy and peace. When
the heathen rage and try to flee from history, attempting to
rewrite and give new dispensations and periodizations within
some artificially constructed idea of history, God is denied and
the human measure itself is lost. The worst set of crimes in the

history of mankind were engineered by Ph.D.'s and committed by baptized Christians. Until the churches have come clean on that massive Event, and stop trying to hide behind the skirts of an occasional Bonhoeffer or Delp, of whom they are not worthy, no amount of abstract reference to "humanity" or universalism will save them from a very specific and particular end: damnation.

That slide into damnation started, like the credibility crisis in Christianity, with Christian lies about the Jewish people, with abandonment of the essential Jewishness of Christianity, with murder of those who could be identified as signal representatives of a counterculture the world hated and most of the baptized betrayed with enthusiasm. The baptized gentiles' apostasy is the most significant religious factor in the present crisis of Christendom. It did not end with the Holocaust. It will not be cured until the churches face with utterly ruthless self-appraisal the meaning of that mass apostasy and trace it to its source. It will take far more than a placid "spirituality" or a flaccid religion of accommodation to make the turn to recovery of integrity and renewal.

To begin the agonizing reappraisal, Christians may study to understand and learn to rejoice in the series of events which have brought the Jewish people out of crucifixion into resurrection. Whether they do so or not will depend upon whether crucifixion and resurrection and "peoplehood" have become for the Christians mere empty words, no longer first-order language. It is time for the Christians to go up to Jerusalem again, not for some vulgar triumphalist missions or patronizing political schemes, but to go back to school.

The Christian betrayal of humanity began with the betrayal of that portion nearest to them: the Jewish people.

> Any man who loves God while hating or despising His creation will in the end hate God. A Jew who rejects his origins, his brothers, to make a so-called contribution to mankind, will in the end betray mankind. That is true of all men.[21]

That is certainly true for Christians, whose accommodation to pagan thought began early and whose cultivation of propositional or "enlightened" Antisemitism has stayed late. The flight into speculative abstractions, the flight from concrete historical events, the anxiety about the essential Jewishness of Christian tradition and belief—all are part of the same spirit of gentile rebellion. And they resulted in our own time in the mass murder of Jews and the mass apostasy of Christians.

NOTES

1. Franklin H. Littell, "The Fall of the Church," in *The Origins of Sectarian Protestantism* (New York: Macmillan Co., 1964).

2. John Lawson, *A Theological and Historical Introduction to the Apostolic Fathers* (New York: Macmillan Co., 1961), pp. 81, 122, 196 f., 274 f.

3. Cyprian: "Three Books of Testimonies Against the Jews," Treatise 12 in volume 13 of *The Ante-Nicene Christian Library*, ed. Roberts and Donaldson (Edinburgh: T. & T. Clark, 1869), pp. 78–198.

4. Cited in Amos Elon, *The Israelis: Founders and Sons* (New York: Holt, Rinehart & Winston, 1971), p. 51.

5. "Declaration on the Relationship of the Church to Non-Christian Religions," in *Commentary on the Documents of Vatican II*, ed. Herbert Vorgrimler (New York: Herder & Herder, 1969), 3:1–136; see also A. Roy Eckardt, *Your People, My People* (New York: Quadrangle, 1974), pp. 49–51.

6. Cf. the very important article by Professor Johan Bouwman, "Die arabische Welt angesichts Israel," VIII *Emuna* (1973) 4:245–62. Among other things, this work by a specialist should help to destroy the false rumor that "the Arabs" are not also susceptible to a virulent Antisemitism with theological roots.

7. Judd Teller, *Scapegoat of Revolution* (New York: Charles Scribner's Sons, 1954), passim.

8. Cf. "How Zionists Manipulate Your News," in *United Church Observer*, March 1972.

9. Loraine Boettner, *The Millennium* (Philadelphia: Presbyterian and Reformed Publ. Co., 1958), p. 311 f.

10. Iona Malachy, "American Fundamentalism and the Holy Land" (provisional title; read in manuscript; publication pending).

11. For the general record, see Hertzel Fishman, *American Protestantism and the Jewish State* (Detroit: Wayne State University Press, 1973), passim.

12. Arnold J. Toynbee, *A Study of History*, abridged by D. C. Somervell (New York: Oxford University Press, 1947), 1:22, 135, 388–89, etc.

13. Cf. Carl Hermann Voss, *Stephen S. Wise: Servant of the People* (Philadelphia: Jewish Publ. Soc'y, 1969), pp. 255–56.

14. Cajus Fabricius, *Positive Christianity in the Third Reich* (Dresden: Püschel, 1937), p. 13.

15. Bernhard E. Olson, *Faith and Prejudice* (New Haven: Yale University Press, 1963), p. 80.

16. Ibid., p. 52.

17. André Lacocque, "Encounter with the Old Testament," 62 *The Chicago Theological Seminary Register* (1972) 2:1.

18. Y. Harkabi, *Arab Attitudes to Israel* (Jerusalem: Israel Universities Press, 1971), pp. 261, 263.

19. George Wesley Buchanan, "Jewish and Christian Relationships," *Religion in Life* (Summer 1971): 279.

20. Fred Gladstone Bratton, *The Crime of Christendom* (Boston: Beacon Press, 1969), pp. 204, 223, 224.

21. Wiesel, *Souls on Fire*, p. 32.

III

THE CHURCH STRUGGLE AND THE JEWS

The German Church Struggle, 1933–45, and parallel conflicts between Christian minorities and totalitarian rule in the Netherlands, Norway, Austria, Denmark, and France has as yet scarcely entered into the thought of the planning committees for church school literature. Perhaps this is just as well for the moment, for misuse and misinterpretation of that encounter would be worse than neglect. When the martyrs and confessors of the Church Struggle are held up to honor without considering at the same time the failure of the churches in the matter of the Holocaust, a spirit of boasting can easily drown out any mood of repentance which might turn us around.

As Arthur Cochrane pointed out in his classic on the Barmen Synod and Confession of Faith, the Church Struggle was "the struggle of the church against the church for the church."[1] This point cannot be made too often, for the cheap and easy view of the Church Struggle is that it was like the persecutions of old in which martyrs and confessors stood to the death against heathenism. And now the purveyors of cheap grace are beginning to use the faithfulness of a few Christians like Dietrich Bonhoeffer to boast of the church's record of courage in the face of the spiritual enemy![2] The truth is that the Church Struggle was fought out within the institutions themselves, not between "insiders" and "outsiders," that most church constituents apostatized and only a small percentage remained faithful, and that most of the theological and ecclesiastical crises which surfaced during this time of trial are yet unresolved.

The question of the meaning of mass apostasy and betrayal has so far been resolved neither by the theological faculties nor by the churches although more progress has been made in West Germany and the Netherlands than elsewhere. And this is of course precisely the reason that the most enlightened and sensitive theologians and churchmen in German and Dutch Catholicism are having trouble with reactionaries in the Curia, who are steadily regaining the ground they lost under good Pope John XXIII. And it is the reason that American Protestant churchmen, leaders in one of the few intact areas of culture-Christianity left in the world, refuse to consider the need for basic church reform. Even while church social action agencies and courageous spokesmen are under heavy fire, and the attackers are making use of their supporters within the denominations, denominational judicatories refuse to consider enforcement of their own official disciplinary standards.

To remember the Church Struggle of an earlier day is painful. The record of most theologians and churchmen, in England and America as well as in the Third Reich, was confused and weak where not outright wicked. The conduct of the masses of baptized Christians covered the scale from enthusiastic apostasy to accommodation. Few indeed were the martyrs and confessors, and their meritorious conduct does not save the rest of us from the need for self-appraisal and repentance and correcting our false teaching and wrongdoing.

Adolf Hitler, the Third Reich, the Aryan paragraphs, and the Death Camps—these were not accidental appearances in the heart of Christendom. They were not strange and inexplicable manifestations of some sudden revolt of demonism, irruptions out of the abyss which defy intelligent appraisal. Neither were they uniquely German and Teutonic, as though some racial explanation might serve to take the curse from the rest of us. They were the legitimate offspring of a "Christian civilization" which, underneath the cosmetics of official creeds and public displays of piety, was formless and heathen at heart. As Alexander Donat, a Jewish survivor, reported the question raised in a Death Camp: "How can Christianity survive the discovery that after a thousand years of its being Europe's official religion,

Europe remains pagan at heart?"[3] That is the key question, and
it has not yet been answered because the churches have not yet
lifted it up to discussion, prayer, and fasting. Therefore, among
other things, it is not yet certain that Christianity can survive.

Even among the churchmen who saw the spiritual treason
and murderous direction of Nazi totalitarianism most clearly,
there was little enough awareness that the heart of the matter
was "the Jewish question." Karl Barth early became the leading
theologian of Protestant resistance, and according to W. A. Visser't Hooft, he was also the leading theologian of the ecumenical movement which came out of the Church Struggle.[4] But
when Eberhard Bethge's great biography was published, Barth
felt moved to write Bonhoeffer's friend and biographer as follows:

> New to me (in your biography) was the fact that Bonhoeffer in 1933
> viewed the Jewish question as the first and decisive question, even
> as the only one, and took it in hand so energetically. I have long felt
> guilty myself that I did not make this problem central, in any case
> not in public, for instance in the two Barmen declarations of 1934
> which I had composed. Certainly, a text in which I inserted a word
> to that effect would not have found agreement in 1934—neither in
> the Reformed Synod of January, 1934; nor in the General Synod of
> May at Barmen. But there is no excuse that I did not fight properly
> for this cause, just because I was caught up in my affairs somewhere
> else.[5]

Another leader, and subsequently historian, of the Church
Struggle, Wilhelm Niemoeller, has written with equal honesty
of the church's failure to get to the critical issue. He opened an
article in 1968 with the words: "It has become evident that the
Jewish question was actually the *key question of the Church
Struggle.* But if we seek the resistance which was raised in the
Protestant Church in this matter, we come to a miserable re-
sult."[6]

If men of such stature, men who have worked tirelessly in the
Church Struggle, can look the churches' failure in the eye and
confess their own shortcomings, why should others hesitate?
The reason seems to be that the same spiritual weakness that
makes some men trimmers and quislings in the hour of decision

makes them suppress the critical issues later. And—as the real leaders of spiritual resistance have been the first to make Christian confession—the churches did fail; most of the church leaders failed, and even the resistance largely failed to understand the signal importance of the rejection of the Jews to the malaise of Christendom.[7]

Genocide: "Pagan" or "Christian"?

It has become popular, among some churchmen and general historians, to deal with nazism as a "pagan" irruption—essentially atavistic, tribal, and anti-Christian. There is much to be said for the argument. An able theologian has even elaborated a thoroughly evidenced and keenly argued proof that Adolf Hitler deliberately developed an *Ersatzreligion* with himself as prophet.[8] Any who remember the "cathedral of lights" which Albert Speer developed, or saw the pagan liturgical dances which often served as prelude to party rallies, or recall the crowd hysteria which responded to the *Führer*'s evangelistic fervor, will find the argument persuasive. The Nazis also developed their holy days, shrines, apotheosis of heroes. A strong case can also be made that both Marxism and nazism are "post-Christian" ideologies, with their theoreticians claiming each system of being to supersede earlier worlds of thought and styles of life.

The trouble with this line of argument is that it relieves the Christians and their leaders of their guilt for what happened. And it puts the whole tragic struggle back into the familiar pattern of persecution (from the outside) directed against faithful Christians. That was not, however, the story of the Church Struggle. The Church Struggle was something new in Christian history; although when masses of the baptized went over to Islam in North Africa in the eighth and ninth centuries, something similar must have occurred. The Church Struggle was a conflict *within* the church between mass movements of apostate and comparatively small minorities of the faithful.

That Church Struggle was not unique to Germany; in fact, it continues throughout Christendom today. Among the younger churches, schisms have been fostered by false leaders serving racist idols and financed by selfish economic interests which oppose the ecumenical movement. In old sections of Christendom like Greece and Spain, the name of Christianity is still invoked to cover brutality, corruption, and oppression. In the United States, the John Birch Society and other reactionary groups have in the last decade and a half seriously injured the churches' drive for racial and economic justice, ecumenical and international peace. Again and again the language of religion has been used to cover the real source of the attacks on religion. In one denomination, the Lutheran Church-Missouri Synod, the language of hyperorthodoxy has been used to cover a putsch that to many seemed anti-Christian in spirit and strategy.

If the churches had used the means of spiritual government at their disposal to call the Nazi leaders to repentance, to return to minimal Christian standards, if the Nazi elite had been excommunicated for failure to respond, then today the churches could say truthfully, "They were pagans. They left our fellowship in the covenant. They were not of us." But the churches did not do this. Instead they retained in their membership and accorded signal honors to traitors to human liberty, mass murderers, and apostate Christians. Adolf Hitler died a Roman Catholic, and an annual mass is celebrated in his memory in Madrid. Hermann Goering died a Lutheran. We Christians cannot come back today and claim no responsibility for what they did in the name of law and order and anti-Bolshevism, claiming to protect "religion."

Those bishops and other church executives who broke their vows to maintain discipline and see to "the form of sound words" cannot come to us now and talk about Nazi "paganism"; nor can any of us professed Christians claim innocence of guilt. As the best of us said at Stuttgart in October, 1945, "We accuse ourselves that we didn't witness more courageously, pray more faithfully, believe more joyously, love more ardently."[9] Of what were they guilty? Of what are we Christians today guilty? Guilty of guilt! In the erosion of Christian fundamentals, even preachers and teachers have fallen into the notion that guilt feelings are wrong and "errors" are only those misdeeds deliberately and individually done. What a runt the once majestic doctrine of "sin" has turned out to be!

Further, any effort to divest the churches of responsibility by categorizing the Nazis as "neopagans" ignores the centuries of false teaching which made the murder of the Jews possible and logical. Christendom was impregnated with hatred of the Jews. Ruth Rouse, who traveled widely for the World's Student Christian Federation from before World War I up to World War II, is as good a witness as any. Listen to her story:

> But bitterer than all "national" questions was the gentile *versus* Jew complex. Anti-Semitism was rampant in the universities throughout the area. The author's experience was typical: When I first addressed women students in Vienna, the lecture room was filled with curious girls: half those present were Jewesses. No one had the faintest doubt that the Federation, as a *Christian* society like all other "Christian" organizations with which they were acquainted would be anti-Semitic and Roman Catholic. The first question asked me, at this meeting was "What do you think of the pogroms (i.e. the massacres of the Jews) in Russia?" and both Gentiles *and* Jews expected me as a "Christian" to express approval.
>
> The spectre of anti-Semitism in continental Europe had always loomed large and showed signs of increasing gravity. When Robert Wilder was about to hold a series of meetings in a certain European country, he was introduced to the head of the Government, who shook him warmly by the hand, exclaiming, "I am delighted to meet a member of the Student Christian Movement, for I too hate the Jews." A long interview followed, in which Robert Wilder made clear that in his view the acid test of real Christianity is the treatment of the Jew.[10]

Before the Holocaust occurred, the spirit of murder, the justification of genocide, was well advanced in Christian circles. Before the Christians win their way back to integrity and credibility, they will have to rely upon something more potent than "cheap grace" to redeem them.

Christians and Jews in Nazi Germany

In a brilliant paper, the friend and biographer of Bonhoeffer, Eberhard Bethge, has distinguished three periods of the German Church Struggle.[11] At first, a period during which a majority of the Protestant clergy rallied to spiritual resistance against the heretics and accommodators *(Deutsche Christen),* the issue was seen as a struggle against heresy in the church. Then, as Nazi government measures invaded the religious realm increasingly, as confessional matters rather than ethical concerns came to dominate the Confessing church, many open supporters fell away; the fiction was maintained for a time that disregard for the church's integrity was due to party underlings. Finally, when it was recognized that loyalty to Christ meant open opposition to the Nazi state and its *Führer,* few held fast; perhaps 20 percent of the pastors stayed consistently with the Confessing church. Bonhoeffer was the only churchman and theologian of front rank who drew the necessary consequences and went into political opposition. He was complicit in conspiracy and attempted overthrow of the regime. He confided in close friends in the ecumenical movement, "I pray for the defeat of my country."[12] But when he walked his lonely way, he did not expect the church to remember him in intercessory prayer as many congregations did those pastors who were imprisoned on clearly Christian (that is, churchly) issues; he felt he must act as a citizen rather than as a churchman when he went into open opposition.

Bonhoeffer refused a job to teach at Union Theological Seminary during the war and returned home (1939), saying that he would have no authority to help rebuild Germany after the defeat unless he shared in the coming miseries of his people. He was murdered by the Nazis just three days before the American troops reached the prison where he was incarcerated. In his writings he had often glimpsed the importance of the "Jewish issue" to the Church Struggle and to sound Christian thought: "The docetic heresy is the typical heresy of Greek thought. It is pagan thought *par excellence.* It has one opponent: Jewish thought."[13] He kept his friendship with persons stigmatized as Jews; he worked to help Jews escape the Third Reich; he said it was wrong for Christians to hurry through the Old Testament to get to the New; he said "only he who cries out for the Jews may sing Gregorian chant";[14] he opposed the Aryan paragraphs in public life and fought against a racist church.

Yet this same Bonhoeffer, martyr and confessor of the faith, was at one time willing to consider separation of the Jews from the German society within the political prerogatives of the government. He accepted the myth that the Christian church supersedes the Jewish people in history.[15] He affirmed the deicide myth:

> Now the measures of the state toward Judaism in addition stand in a special context for the church. The church of Christ has never lost sight of the thought that the 'chosen people', who nailed the redeemer of the world to the cross, must bear the curse for its action through a long history of suffering. . . . The conversion of Israel, that is to be the end of the people's period of suffering.[16]

The sad truth is that Bonhoeffer was much better than his theology. The man who fought Hitler as a citizen but not as a churchman was better than his theological tradition; if his church had provided an adequate social ethic, he would have fought the tyrant in the name of God. The man whose humanity and decency led him to run risks for Jews and to oppose practical Antisemitism was better than the bad theology which laid the foundations for Christian Antisemitism.

The faithful Christian minority among Roman Catholic churchmen was crippled by the same corpus of false teaching about the Jews and the same lack of adequate commentaries on the right of resistance. In 1933 Cardinal Faulhaber preached five Advent sermons in Munich, addressing large crowds in defense of the Old Testament and in attack on an Aryanized Christianity. He even attacked the old Teutonic heathenism and the new German Faith Movement and concluded that "a falling away from Christianity, a falling back into heathenism, would be the beginning of the end of the German nation."[17] Yet he felt compelled to reaffirm that "after the death of Christ, Israel was dismissed from service to revelation,"[18] and to make several other traditional statements denigrating the Jews.

Only at one point—when the Nazis set out to put to death all institutionalized defectives—did Roman Catholic leaders like Faulhaber and von Galen join with Protestant leaders like Bodelschwingh and Wurm to promote a massive defiance of a decree of the regime. Nothing was done by either church, except on a purely fortuitous and individual and clandestine basis,

on the greatest crime of all: the setting up of Death Camps and
the murder of six million Jews.

In the common sector of Christianity, where the faith was
rarely deep enough to produce any serious conflicts with Nazi
thought and action, Antisemitism was not even partially inhib-
ited. After a careful study of the Roman Catholic leadership,
Gordon Zahn was brought to state:

> . . . the German Catholic who looked to his religious superiors for
> spiritual guidance and direction regarding service in Hitler's wars
> received virtually the same answers he would have received from
> the Nazi ruler himself.[19]

From the total record, he drew the general principle which can
be applied to all kinds of unformed culture-religion:

> To the extent that the Church does accommodate itself to a secular
> regime, it becomes, in effect, an agent of that regime, supplement-
> ing the secular controls with those of the spiritual order.[20]

Zahn was subject to all kinds of personal and professional attack
by defenders of the German Catholic establishment because he
had exposed the facts of the church's failure to view. But far
more biting is the question put by a German Catholic nobleman
who was, after the war, a member of the parliament in Bonn:
"Where were the German bishops when the Concordat was
signed, and the Church in Germany surrendered millions of
loyal Catholics to Nazi terror?"[21] The answer to that question
is unfortunately well known: they were capitulating. And the
Concordat between the Nazi government and the papal see,
which gave Hitler his first major diplomatic victory and entrance into "decent" international society, was engineered by
the man who later became Pope Pius XII.

On the Protestant side, large sections of the churchmen made
no effort even to preserve the Jewish foundations of the faith,
let alone to show concern for the fate of living Jews. Collaborating synods denounced the Confessing church for "fundamentalism," for "lack of patriotism," for "internationalism" dangerous
to German national identity *(Volksgemeinschaft)*. The *Deutsche Christen* announced a new historical dispensation: "In the
person of the *Führer* we behold the One sent from God, who

places Germany in the presence of the Lord of History . . ."[22] They said it was Hitler who had translated Christianity out of theory into unique *praxis.*[23] And they went on to affirm an identity of nazism and Christianity: "We German Christians are the first trenchline of National Socialism. . . . To live, fight and die for Adolf Hitler means to say Yes to the path of Christ."[24] A special edition of the four gospels was published free of Jewish influence because "Zionism has to disappear from the liturgy and the song-material."[25] (Feeling themselves to be winning, these Antisemites apparently saw no reason to work out theoretical distinctions between *Zionism* and *Judaism!*)

In the meantime, the Confessing church went its increasingly difficult way. For a time two underground seminaries functioned to train young men who wished to avoid the theological faculties corrupted by Nazi thought control. Many young pastors were drafted, their clerical status not recognized by the government and the church offices the government controlled. Many more volunteered for the Eastern front, finding it a relief to be engaged in "the fight against communism" and to be delivered from the desperate ambiguities of life in the resistance. One of the most tragic figures of all was Kurt Gerstein, whose life and death show those ambiguities to the full measure.

Kurt Gerstein was, like Martin Niemoeller and other strong resisters, at first uncertain whether the Nazi party represented national renewal or disaster. He too was disenchanted early and was twice arrested and jailed by the Gestapo for making speeches and distributing pamphlets as a youth leader of the Confessing church. Later he managed to join the SS, for the express purpose, he confided to a few friends, of penetrating and unmasking the organization which the year before (1940) had applied euthanasia to thousands of inmates of German insane asylums. Gerstein's own sister-in-law had been among the victims. Because he was trained in both engineering and medicine, he was rapidly advanced in responsibility and finally became involved in the project to deliver and use Zyklon B in the extermination camps. Twice he witnessed gas chambers in operation, and he made several fruitless efforts to rouse the Allies and the German people against the developing Holocaust. His

approaches, both to government legations and to church officials (including the Papal Nuncio in Berlin), were of no avail.

Gerstein's account of one shipment can now be validated by
comparison with a huge volume of published and unpublished
public documents.

> The first train came in . . . 45 freight-cars containing 6,700 persons,
> 1,450 of whom were already dead on arrival. Behind the small,
> barbed-wire openings, one saw pale-faced children, men, women,
> with the marks of great fright etched in their faces . . . the people
> [are driven] out of the freight-cars with leather whips. Then,
> through a huge loud-speaker instructions are given: "Undress com-
> pletely, give up false teeth and glasses . . . hand in all valuables and
> money" . . . without receipt. Then the women and girls to the
> barber, who cuts off their hair in one or two quick strokes. . . . Then
> the march begins: to the right and left, barbed-wire; behind, two
> dozen . . . guns. . . . Completely naked they march by, men, women,
> girls, children, babies, even one-legged persons supported by the
> others, all naked. In one corner, a giant SS-man tells these unfortu-
> nates in a soothing voice: "Nothing whatever will happen to you. All
> you have to do is to breathe deeply, it strengthens the lungs; this
> inhalant . . . is a very good disinfectant." . . . For a few of those poor
> innocents, this offers a faint flicker of hope, just enough to make
> them march on without resisting into the death chambers. . . . Then
> they walk up the little staircase—and see the truth! Nursing mothers
> with babies at their breasts, naked; numerous children of all ages,
> naked too; they hesitate, but they enter the gas chambers, most of
> them silently, pushed by those behind them, driven by the whips of
> the SS-men. A Jewess of about 40 years, with eyes aflame, calls down
> on the heads of the assassins all of the innocent blood shed here.
> . . . Many pray, others ask: "Who will wash us in death?"
>
> I prayed with them . . . crying aloud to their God and mine
> . . . [unheard because of the] great noise all around me. I would have
> willingly entered that gas chamber; I would have liked to die there
> with them. But if my corpse in SS officer's uniform had been found
> there, nobody would have assumed that I had died in protest against
> these murders. . . . My death would have been regarded as an
> accident, and my epitaph would have been: "Died in the service of
> his beloved Führer." It could not be. I had no right to yield to the
> temptation to die among these people. . . . I must live to testify to
> what I had seen, and to bring charges against the murderers. . . .
> After 32 minutes, finally all are dead. . . . Like basalt pillars the dead

still stand, for there is neither room to fall nor collapse. Even in death, families can be recognized still clasping hands.[26]

Kurt Gerstein committed suicide in 1945 after performing his self-assigned mission "to bear witness." Of Pius XII, who received Gerstein's report in August, 1942, the papal secretary wrote: "It was difficult for the Pope to satisfy both sides, the Jews and Allied public opinion."[27]

How is Kurt Gerstein to be remembered in the church calendar? Is he to be listed with the Jewish victims of nazism and its vociferous or silent allies? The liturgy of one Jewish congregation at Yom Kippur, 1969, commended him to recognition and prayers as one of the "righteous of the nations of the world." When the churches once face the meaning of the Holocaust, will the saints of this age include a Christian theologian who became a conspirator against the government of his country and a Christian layman who became a conspirator in the SS and then a witness at Nuremberg and finally a suicide? Surely this is less absurd to contemplate than the thought that a churchman of privilege, who helped Hitler to power and never once embarrassed him, should go on the calendar as a "saint"!

A New Martyrology

At Yad Vashem, the international memorial and research center to the Holocaust in Jerusalem, there is a pathway called *l'Avenue des Justes*. Trees are planted there, each dedicated to the memory of a gentile proven to have saved the life of at least one Jew. It is a small and select company. In the chancy survival of persons and documents in a totalitarian state, some who saved Jews are not memorialized on the avenue, and many who were martyred as opponents of Third Reich policies, including Antisemitic decrees, saved no Jewish life directly. There is a remarkable dearth of churchmen; most are common folk, remembered for this alone.

The reasons rescuers have given vary greatly.[28] A Bulgarian statesman, Dimo Kazasov, put it in language evoking memories of what the Old Testament teaches about righteousness: "I did what I did because I do not believe that a nation that abandons its moral and human values has the right to exist."[29]

A Dutchman, Joop Westerweel, member of the Plymouth Brethren and a martyr, summed up the decision in this way:

> Anybody who takes part in the persecution of the Jews, whether voluntarily or against his will, is looking for an excuse for himself. Some cannot give up a business deal, others are doing it for the sake of their families; and the Jewish professors must disappear without protest for the sake of the university.
>
> I have to go through these difficult days without breaking, but in the end my fate will be decided and I shall go like a man.[30]

We are reminded of the determined affirmation of Dr. Ringelblum, historian of the Warsaw ghetto, who perished there: "Let it be said that though we have been sentenced to death and know it, we have not lost our human features . . ."[31]

Both martyrs, Christian (Westerweel) and Jewish (Ringelblum), knew a great truth that the trimmers and accommodators missed: the dehumanization of other human persons is only acceptable to those who have themselves lost human features. The generalized excuses for spiritual treason are many and resounding: "for the good of the state," "to protect the church," "to obey orders faithfully," "to build a strong ethnic community," "to keep religion out of politics," "to render to Caesar that which is Caesar's," and so forth. But the same persons who denied that any rulers were more than men and could ride like heathen gods over the bodies of others would not for themselves choose a role less than human.

There were some Jews who lost their dignity and integrity in obsequious appeals to those at the controls of the murder machine. Thus a daughter-in-law of Karl Kautsky wrote the Nazi authorities begging for a permit for family emigration on the basis that they had never belonged to the Jewish community.[32] But the Adversary knew the Jew even when he had forgotten or denied himself and his people. In the words of a contemporary, "It is a sad compliment to the Jews that no totalitarianism, whether of the left or the right, can afford their presence."[33] The Jew could not disappear; his offense was nothing more or less than the fact that he was there. But what of the Christians? What of the smooth churchmen who made their peace with the

Adversary, retreating into the prehistory of their prebaptismal condition, even while they found a form of words to cover with pious phrases their loss of human face?

To this day the churches have not dealt with the truth that the mark of Cain is on their foreheads, that, not just to Jews and skeptical humanists, but to many of their own "members" Christianity has become incredible because of them. Jesus of Nazareth, a Jew, is honored far beyond the boundary of Christianity, in other religions and ideologies; Christianity is in dispute even among the baptized, especially among youth and students, and it is our own wickedness that has created the credibility gap. When shall our church school studies, our sermons, our prayers and hymns, begin to reveal the kind of spiritual wrestling by which a murderer may out of the long night win the Lord's blessing?

> Come, O thou Traveler unknown,
> Whom still I hold, but cannot see;
> My company before is gone,
> And I am left alone with thee;
> With thee all night I mean to stay,
> And wrestle till the break of day.
>
> I need not tell thee who I am;
> My sin and misery declare . . .[34]

For the time being, until the Christians have learned again to recognize and to honor the Name, it is enough for them to reflect upon a powerful truth: in the triumph of anti-Christian ideologies, parties, and systems in the twentieth century, supported enthusiastically by the vast majority of apostate baptized, the Jewish people has supplied by far the largest number of martyrs and witnesses to the God of Abraham, Isaac, and Jacob. He is also the Christians' God, when they remember who they are. But most of the baptized have suppressed the memory in the time of testing, whether in the rise of nazism in Germany or in the triumph of culture-religion in America today. And few indeed, thus far, are the theologians and churchmen willing to draw the knife to win Isaac. Our church conferences and publishing houses display a veritable whirlwind of fads and fancies; our boards and agencies run from one enthusiasm to the next.

But who will wrestle through the long night, injured as we are,
until there appears again the face of a Man, illumined by the
light of God?

NOTES

1. Arthur C. Cochrane, *The Church's Confession under Hitler* (Philadelphia:
Westminster Press, 1962), p. 19.

2. Cf. for example the *United Church* (of Canada) *Observer*, November 1971,
in which Bonhoeffer's martyrdom is used to reproach critics of the church's
record toward the Jewish people and the absurd claim is made that the Allies
("we"!) went to war to save the Jews.

3. Alexander Donat, *The Holocaust Kingdom* (New York: Holt, Rinehart &
Winston, 1965), pp. 230–31.

4. Willem A. Visser't Hooft, *Die Welt war meine Gemeinde* (Munich: R. Piper
& Co., 1972), p. 423 f. Bonhoeffer wrote: "The German church struggle marks
the second great stage in the history of the ecumenical movement and will in
a decisive way be normative for its future." *No Rusty Swords*, ed. Edwin H.
Robertson, trans. Edwin H. Robertson and John Bowden (New York: Harper &
Row, 1965), p. 326. Cf. also Franklin H. Littell, "Die Bedeutung des Kirchen-
kampfes für die Ökumene," 20 *Evangelische Theologie* (1960) 1:1–21.

5. E. Bethge in 28 *Evangelische Theologie* (1968) 10:555. According to a
recent comprehensive study of the Confessing Church and the Jews, it was
already clear by November of 1933 that the organized Christian resistance
would stress the dogmatic rather than the ethical base of opposition, that is,
would go with Barth rather than Bonhoeffer; thereby the question of the treatment of the Jews (and others consigned to concentration camps or death camps)
was relegated to secondary importance. Wolfgang Gerlach, "Zwischen Kreuz
und Davidstern" (Ph.D. diss., University of Hamburg, 1972), pp. 492–96.

6. Wilhelm Niemoeller, "Ist die Judenfrage 'bewältigt'?" *Beiheft* of *Junge
Kirche* (May 1968).

7. The very few in the resistance, like Freiherr von Pechmann and Bonhoeffer, who glimpsed the centrality of the issue were driven more and more into
personal isolation—even from their friends. Cf. Gerlach, "Zwischen Kreuz und
Davidstern," pp. 194–96.

8. Michael D. Ryan, "Hitler's Challenge to the Churches: A Theological Political Analysis of *Mein Kampf*," in *The German Church Struggle and the Holocaust*, ed. Franklin H. Littell and Hubert G. Locke (Detroit: Wayne State
University Press, 1974).

9. For the Stuttgart Declaration, see Franklin H. Littell, *The German Phoenix*
(New York: Doubleday & Co., 1960), app. C.

10. Ruth Rouse, *The World's Student Christian Federation . . . the First Thirty
Years* (London: SCM Press, 1948), pp. 166, 271–72.

11. Eberhard Bethge, "Troubled Self-Interpretation and Uncertain Recep-

tion in the Church Struggle," in *The German Church Struggle and the Holocaust*.

12. Visser't Hooft, *Die Welt war meine Gemeinde*, p. 186.

13. Dietrich Bonhoeffer, *Christ the Center* (New York: Harper & Row, 1966), p. 79.

14. Quoted in Eberhard Bethge, *Dietrich Bonhoeffer* (New York: Harper & Row, 1970), p. 512.

15. Bonhoeffer, *No Rusty Swords*, p. 241.

16. Ibid., p. 226.

17. (Cardinal) Faulhaber, *Judentum/ Christentum/ Germanentum* (Munich: A. Huber, 1934), p. 103.

18. Ibid., p. 10.

19. Gordon C. Zahn, *German Catholics and Hitler's Wars* (New York: Sheed & Ward, 1962), p. 17.

20. Ibid., p. 216.

21. Prince Hubertus zu Loewenstein, *Towards the Further Shore: An Autobiography* (London: Victor Gollancz, 1968), p. 135.

22. Kurt Meier, *Die Deutschen Christen* (Göttingen: Vandenhoeck & Ruprecht, 1964), p. 8.

23. Ibid., p. 234.

24. Ibid., p. 194.

25. Ibid., p. 292.

26. Nuremberg Document PS–1553 in the National Archives. The writer wishes to express his thanks to Dr. Robert Wolfe for this and other study helps. For a list of the principal documents and microfilmed records of the Nazi party and state as they relate to the Church Struggle, see the notes to John S. Conway, "The Present State of Research and Writing on the Church Struggle," in *The German Church Struggle and the Holocaust*, pp. 293–94. For a critical appraisal of materials on the Holocaust, see Henry Friedlander, "Publications on the Holocaust," ibid., pp. 69–94.

27. "Pius XII and the Third Reich," 30 *Look* (1966) 10:46. For a careful study of the relations of Pius XII and the Nazi regime, see Saul Friedländer, *Pius XII and the Third Reich: A Documentation* (London: Chatte & Windus, 1966).

28. Professor Manfred Wolfson of Sacramento State College has been studying German rescuers of Jews and has published several articles on the subject.

29. Ariah L. Bauminger, *Roll of Honour* (Tel Aviv: "Hamanova" Publishing House, 1971), introduction.

30. Ibid., pp. 51–52.

31. Jacob Sloan, ed. and trans., *The Journal of Emmanuel Ringelblum*, (New York: McGraw-Hill Book Co., 1958), p. 299.

32. J. C. Presser, *The Destruction of the Dutch Jews* (New York: E. P. Dutton & Co., 1969), p. 219.

33. Lee Katcher, "The Vanishing Jews of East Germany," 3 *Dimensions* (1968) 1:34.

34. Charles Wesley.

IV

THE MEANING OF THE HOLOCAUST

Sensitive Jewish writers like Elie Wiesel and Emil Fackenheim have warned us against applying too facile explanations to the Holocaust and drawing too ready conclusions from it. The warning is especially pertinent for those whose normal intellectual discourse strains toward abstractions, generalizations, and rules. Certainly the warning must be heeded by gentiles, and when it comes from men who personally experienced the terrors of "the Final Solution," common decency commends silence. But the mind is drawn back repeatedly to the evidence of *the mass murder of Jews by Christians in the heart of Christendom.* Silence becomes impossible. Unless events are meaningless, in which case the biblical world view must be rejected as false, the compulsion to read the signs rests heavily upon any who think and feel.

One alternative has been presented by Richard Rubenstein, after what is certainly one of the most dramatic confrontations reported in contemporary theological literature. Let him tell his own story:

> On August 17, 1961, at 4:30 in the afternoon, I had a two-hour conversation with Probst Dr. Heinrich Grüber at his home in Berlin-Dahlem. Dean Grüber had been the only German to testify in Jerusalem against Adolf Eichmann at the celebrated trial earlier that summer. He had a distinguished record in the defense of Jewish

rights, or at least, the right of Christians of "non-Aryan" origin, during the Nazi period. He had himself been a concentration camp inmate. We talked under almost apocalyptic conditions. American army tanks rumbled outside his home. He was pastor of a church in East Berlin. Living in West Berlin he was very upset that he was cut off from his flock. He began to use the imagery of the biblical theology of history to describe what was happening.

God was punishing a sinful Germany, he declared. He asserted that God was making Germans refugees as the Germans had made others homeless. Having commenced with his biblical interpretation of recent history, he could not stop until he asserted that it had been God's will to send Adolf Hitler to exterminate Europe's Jews. At the moment that I heard Grüber make that assertion, I had what was perhaps the most important single crisis of faith I have ever had. I recognized that Grüber was not an Antisemite and that his assertion that the God of the Covenant was and is the ultimate Author of the great events of Israel's history was no different from the faith of any traditional Jew. Grüber was applying the logic of Covenant Theology to the events of the twentieth century. I appreciated his fundamental honesty. He recognized that, if one takes the biblical theology of history seriously, Adolf Hitler is no more nor less an instrument of God's wrath than Nebuchadnezzar.

. . . I have had to decide whether to affirm the existence of a God who inflicts Auschwitz on his guilty people or to insist that nothing the Jews did made them more deserving of Auschwitz than any other people, that Auschwitz was in no sense a punishment, and that a God who could or would inflict such punishment does not exist. In other words, I have elected to accept what Camus has rightly called the courage of the absurd, the courage to live in a meaningless, purposeless Cosmos rather than believe in a God who inflicts Auschwitz on his people.[1]

Probst Grüber, as Rabbi Rubenstein affirmed, was one of the great men of the Christian resistance to Hitler. Yet the harsh, propositional lines which he drew from biblical orthodoxy repelled rather than commended the living God. Moreover, there was a heavy taint of abstraction—as there often is with dehydrated forms of religion. When he spoke as a German of the German experience, Probst Grüber spoke authentically. When he spoke abstractly, propositionally, about the Jewish experience, he was no longer a bona fide witness. He forgot who he was, to whom he was speaking. Most serious in a Christian pastor, he forgot that the first question as to when to speak and when to keep silent is the question of how the hearer will be helped and the truth thereby served.

Probst Grüber was even then a venerable old man, and he had earned the right to make mistakes. Nothing this writer could say, and nothing Dr. Rubenstein wished to report, could reduce the fact that Probst Grüber was a faithful Christian churchman during long years when such were in very short supply.

But somewhere between treating events as absurd incidents and reading a harsh orthodoxy into them, a way needs be found for a walk of faith that practices a vital dialogue with the past and looks for the Kingdom to come. A sign pointing to that way is the tale or story. Probst Grüber had a far more important story to tell than a host of disciples of Ahimaaz, who like to talk all right, but have nothing to say, having never been where the action was (2 Samuel 18:22–23). But, caught in that moment in the heat of religious abstraction, he turned to the language of propositional orthodoxy and forgot the person listening and the story to be told.

We can learn much from that Jewish tradition which has not only encouraged the debate with God but revitalized the parables and allegories and tales that are so much closer to the heart of biblical truth than any logic and syllogisms and balanced mechanical models. Martin Buber has told of a rabbi whose grandfather was a disciple of the Baal Shem Tov, founder of Hassidism. Once upon a time, when the rabbi was asked to tell a story, he said:

> A story must be told in such a way that it constitutes help in itself. My grandfather was lame. Once they asked him to tell a story about his teacher. And he related how the holy Baal Shem used to hop and dance while he prayed. My grandfather rose as he spoke, and he was so swept away by his story that he himself began to hop and dance to show how the master had done. From that hour on he was cured of his lameness. That's the way to tell a story.[2]

The reported signs of the Messiah are these: that the blind recover their sight, that the lame walk, that the captives are freed. Nowhere is it recorded that one of the signs is this, that the preachers and teachers give consistent answers to philosophical questions.

Fundamental to the mystery, too, is the truth that a Jew has to choose to be a pagan, while the gentile has to choose not to be. Grüber's orthodoxy and Rubenstein's "paganism" are both more acceptable than the frivolity of those who will not recognize the time of their visitation, who have healed the hurt of the daughter of God's people slightly, who are not humbled even unto this day! Even today—with few blessed exceptions—the same posture of triumphalism rules the centers of church bureaucracy; the same lies are told about the Jewish people; the same impatient rejection of repentance and reform prevails; the same unreflective hostility to Israel rules the so-called Christian councils.

When the General Assembly of the World Council of Churches was held at Evanston in 1954, some delegates who had learned the lessons of the Church Struggle sought a clear statement of friendship on the relationship of the Christian churches to the Jewish people. Dutch, German, and French delegates were particularly insistent. On April 27, 1950, for example, the synod of the Evangelical Church in Germany had declared: " . . . by dereliction of duty and in keeping silent we also are guilty of the crimes committed . . . towards the Jews. . . . We pray all Christians to rid themselves of all antisemitism whatsoever, to resist it earnestly where it raises its head again."[3] They remembered past days. So too did the leader of the delegation from the French Reformed Church, whose then president (Marc Boegner) had in 1942 written the chief rabbi of Paris: "Our Church has authorized me to convey to you our feelings of embitterment and disgust at the racist laws which have been introduced in our country."[4] But the appeals of Charles P. Taft of Cincinnati and Charles Malik of Lebanon overcame the appeals of Berkhof and Maury and helped to prevent even a traditional statement about Christian indebtedness to "the Old Israel" from being adopted.

Visser't Hooft's summary of the situation is keenly perceptive:

What was going on behind all this? During the decisive vote, as I watched from the podium how the national delegations voted, I said to myself: the spirit of Hitler walks to and fro here, and up and down. Not as though one or the other was innoculated with Hitlerite Antisemitism. Things hung together in quite another way. I could see that the churchmen from countries which had been subjected for a shorter or longer time to National Socialist rule were almost all convinced that Israel had a central place not only in the previous but also in the future history of salvation. He who had experienced the satanic hatred against the Jews, for him the Pauline interpretation of the fate of Israel in the ninth, tenth and eleventh chapters of the Epistle to the Romans had a deep meaning. The others, who did not know the terrible drama of the destruction of European Jewry from their own observation, did not share this view of things. For them, every singling out of the Jews, every designation of a special historical role, remained in spite of the best intentions a kind of discrimination. Together with the little batch of Middle East Christians, who feared political misunderstandings, they made up the majority vote.[5]

This is precisely the problem in the ecumenical councils today: the lessons of the Holocaust and even the Church Struggle have not been mastered in most churches; the terrible guilt of Christendom and its centuries of false teaching about the Jews has only been admitted by those who learned of Nazi ideology and practice at first hand, and the tiny Christian ghettos in the Muslim world are primarily controlled by political considerations. With the rise of the "Third World" myth, the ecumenical movement and its chief organs are even less inclined to make the ruthless self-assessment and take the corrective measures necessary to reestablish Christian credibility. In America, where the delusions of nineteenth-century culture-religion are still regnant, only the impact of the preliminary stage of a new church struggle has served to move some churchmen to reflection and reappraisal.

The most significant practical results of a beginning reassessment in America have so far been threefold: (1) the release of a "Statement to Our Fellow Christians" by a working party of Roman Catholic, Protestant, and Orthodox theologians;[6] (2) the founding of "Christians Concerned for Israel," a voluntary fellowship with an occasional newsletter;[7] (3) an Annual Scholars' Conference on the Church Struggle and the Holocaust.[8] But the crucial long-range question is how the Christians are to reestablish their credibility vis-à-vis humanity, signalized in the concrete historical situation by the way they rework their relationship to the Jewish people. The Holocaust was the consummation of centuries of false teaching and practice, and until the churches come clean on this "model" situation, very little they have to say about the plight of other victimized and helpless persons or groups will carry authority. There is a symbolic line from Auschwitz to Mylai, but what the churches have to say about Mylai will not be heard until their voice is clear on Auschwitz. The tune must be played backward, the ball of scattered twine must be rolled up through the difficult and mysterious byways of the maze, before we come again into a blessed daylight of faith.

Finally, the meaning of the Holocaust for Christians must be built into the confessions of faith and remembered in the hymns and prayers. That was the turn in the road that most of the churches missed, and many of them are still plodding down a dead-end trail that leads away from the Kingdom of God. We Christians must go back to the turn in the road and reject the signs and signals which, expressing a spiritual and intellectual teaching which was false though familiar, turned us toward Auschwitz.

Nor is it enough to take the right turn for the sake of the church. Karl Barth was quite right in criticizing the Confessing church in 1936 for having shown no sympathy for the millions suffering injustice, for speaking out always on her own behalf. The theologian who condemned the church's seeking to gain her own soul also sensed and defined, though not as strongly as he later wished, the fatal error: "The question of the Jews is the questions of Christ."[9] "Anti-Semitism is sin against the Holy Ghost."[10] Right! For Christians, Antisemitism is not just a peculiarly nasty form of race prejudice; Antisemitism is blasphemy— a much more serious matter!

When the Christians denied their obligations to the Jews, the way to boasting and triumphalism was opened wide, and most

churchmen are still marching cheerfully through it. Even the
Confessing church, though it came closer to the issue than most,
spoke no clear word for the Jews at the Barmen Synod (1934)
and never mentioned the Holocaust in the Stuttgart Declaration of Guilt (1945)!

The Christians must draw the knife on their own Antisemitism for the sake of the truth, not to save the church but for love
of Jesus of Nazareth and his people. There remains far too much
of cunning and calculation, even among Christians well disposed toward the Jews. For example, a fine churchman has
recently called on Christians and Jews to unite against the
"secularism" which reduces all religious mysteries: "Believing
Christians and believing Jews, living on their isolated islands,
have been battered by a sea of unbelievers. We must build a
bridge between those islands."[11] This is not good enough: (1) It
is calculating, whereas brotherhood-love is spontaneous and
unbounded. (2) It presupposes a parity of guilt and goodwill
between the "islands." As a matter of fact, the relationship of
Christendom to the Jewish people has been so wretched for so
long that a number of outspoken Jewish leaders say frankly that
they expect nothing and desire nothing from the Christians
except that they keep their distance. We must earn our way
back to the right to build a bridge, and that requires a flood of
fraternal and loving actions of which we have so far proven
quite incapable. (3) Finally, we need each other to be sure, but
we Christians need Jewry first. The Jewish people can define
itself in history without Christianity: Christians cannot establish
a self-identity except in relationship to the Jewish people—past
and present, and whenever the Christians have attempted to do
so, they have fallen into grievous heresy and sin.

The Problem of Heresy

While rights and liberties usually are close enough to the
historical process to be specified, terms like *humanity* and *freedom* are abstractions that lend themselves readily to cloudy
thinking. License is but freedom run wild, while religious liberty, for example, is a very concrete right; the great champions

of that right, the confrontations that strengthened it, and the documents that define it—all are specific and historical, and stories can be told about them.

The passion of the Enlightenment for abstractions, generalizations, and propositions and the hostility of the "enlightened" to the earthy, finite, and particular have produced a contempt for history and the unique event that has increasingly devitalized the language and dehumanized the word person. Thus it has come about that the worst crimes against human persons have been calculated, scientifically mounted programs, executed in the name of "humanity," "the new man," and "social progress." And the most un-Christian and anti-Christian actions have been justified by "Christian" theories and propositions that have taken leave of the human measure.

The application of mathematical formulae and models, the very "objectivity" and detachment which have contributed so much in the hard sciences, have led to Auschwitz, Babi Yar, the massacre in the Katyn forest, and the atrocity at Mylai. A common misstatement of the problem is that "science" is neutral and crimes are committed when science escapes the control of the humanities. The real problem is that a single pattern of thinking has become normative in sociology as well as chemistry, in political science as well as engineering, in theology as well as nuclear physics. A prideful contempt for the human person, his present condition and his past experience, stains the thoughts and visions of "modern man." Each age has been "the modern age" in turn, of course, but only in the last two centuries has the contempt for history and the lessons of past human experience become obsessive.

In a fine essay Karl Kupisch has described the collapse of historical consciousness. He shows that, although the awakening of the historical sense was the most important intellectual event in Germany after the Reformation, the Nazis began the swindle of historical relativism. Then since the war the motto has been "history-lessness," which leaves in the Third Reich and today nothing but the naked struggle for power.[12] The problem began earlier than the Third Reich, however, and it today affects circles far wider: Liberalism (abstractions), Fundamentalism (propositions), Marxism (dialectical dogmatics), and the whole body of modern thought. It derives from the relentless use of a single style of discourse, whereas the varied levels of human experience and thought are not exhausted even when all possible idioms are used.

The Jewish people is not only a discordant note in the "modern age" because the Jews stand for counterculture, but also because the Jews appear in Western history as carriers of a sense of history, a sense of history which is, among other things, "built upon a realization that the events of history are unique."[13] The flight from history has expressed itself in a number of ways prejudicial to the Jewish people. Emil Fackenheim, in his great essay denying a posthumous victory to Hitler, has summarized the common response to the historical event of the Holocaust: "Rather than face Auschwitz, men everywhere seek refuge in generalities, comfortable precisely because they are generalities. And such is the extent to which reality is shunned that no cries of protest are heard even when in the world community's own forum obscene comparisons are made between Israeli soldiers and Nazi murderers."[14]

But refusal to face honestly the reality of the Holocaust is not the beginning of the treason of the intellectuals and the moral cowardice of many churchmen. It simply exposes in extreme form the final consequences of an obsessive devotion to the dehumanized mechanical model, especially when applied to human experience and human commitments.

In his great classic, *The New Science of Politics,* Eric Voegelin showed how the flight from history has marked modern thought and brought it to internal bankruptcy and external subservience to the gods who rule over the spirit of the times. Internally, intellectual disciplines were corrupted as the quantitative and methodological triumphed over ultimate values:

> As a consequence, all propositions concerning facts will be promoted to the dignity of science, regardless of their relevance, as long as they result from a correct use of method. Since the ocean of facts is infinite, a prodigious expansion of science in the sociological sense becomes possible . . .

Much deeper than by the easily recognized accumulation of trivialities has science been destroyed by the second manifestation of positivism, that is, by the operation on relevant materials under defective theoretical principles. Highly respectable scholars have invested an immense erudition into the digestion of historical materials, and their effort has gone largely to waste because their principle of selection and interpretation had no proper theoretical foundation but derived from the *Zeitgeist*, political preferences, or personal idosyncrasies.[15]

He then went on to show how the mechanization, the abandonment of principles, the relativization of truth(s), worked out in practical politics:

The death of the spirit is the price of progress. Nietzsche revealed this mystery of the Western apocalypse when he announced that God was dead and that He had been murdered. This Gnostic murder is constantly committed by the men who sacrifice God to civilization.

Totalitarianism, defined as the existential rule of Gnostic activists, is the end form of progressive civilization.[16]

In a later work, Voegelin brilliantly demonstrated how Toynbee's great scheme of "history" represents in fact a flight from history into abstractions, and thereby utterly misconstrues the crucial biblical events which form the basis of biblical faith.[17] Toynbee's appraisal of the Jewish people and dislike of Israel, which have surprised and shocked some of his admirers, are but logically consistent outworkings of his speculative presuppositions.

Nazism was in no sense a revolt against "religion" and "spirituality." Neither was it "secularistic." Quite the contrary: in its central creed the party affirmed a devotion to *positives Christentum*. The *Führer* and other party orators made constant reference to "divine providence," "spiritual renewal," "moment of decision," "immortal destiny." "Christian front against materialism," and the like. Many of the party hymns were simply new words written to popular gospel songs, with the same brass bands marching and evoking from crowds the same emotional response. The key question, and here the issue of "heresy" arises, is why the millions of baptized and confirmed Christians had no sense that they were now responding to visions and programs antithetical to biblical faith.

The answer is that most church leaders and theologians had already cast off any binding obedience to what the Bible teaches in stories and precepts and had relativized and adapted what they still retained to fit patriotic and ethnic claims. The common folk received little help from such leaders to distinguish between "religious devotion" and Christian faithfulness.

The net cast for the unwary was large. An early pamphlet by the Deputy *Führer* affirmed: "It is of course obvious that a party member and National Socialist would never describe himself as without faith since the National Socialist ideology presumes a religious attitude."[18] But what was the intellectual and confessional content of that "faith" and that "religious attitude"? As Hans Buchheim showed in his fine study of "religion" in the Third Reich, the unformed religious emotion might flow into any one of three great channels of popular religion—only one of which was vaguely Christian.[19]

The inner circle expressed the religious devotion that Hitler aroused in many of the faithful: "A star shines leading me from deep misery! I am his to the end. My last doubts have disappeared. Germany will live! *Heil Hitler!*"[20] Hitler's loyal churchmen responded in kind. A council of Lutheran leaders (including Werner Ehlert and Paul Althaus), meeting at Ansbach shortly after the Barmen Synod called the church to resistance to nazism, set forth their repudiation of Christian resistance and affirmation of accommodation:

> . . . the unchangeable will of God meets us in the total reality of our life as it is illumined by God's revelation. It binds everyone . . . to the natural orders to which we are subject such as family, nation, race. . . . In this knowledge we thank God the Lord that he has given to our people in its need a Leader (Hitler) as a "pious and faithful sovereign."[21]

Barmen had shown Christianity and National Socialism to be irreconcilable; these churchmen were determined to accommodate a corrupted Christianity to nazism, and to do it in lan-

guage which sounded pious and traditional. The verbosity of
the original German, with its prideful and rotund phrases,
comes through even in translation.

Hitler and Bormann, for their part, intended the liquidation
of the churches in due season.[22] Hitler's "table talk" and the
hidden creed of the movement were explicit enough:

> The more accurately we recognize and observe the law of nature
> and life . . . so much the more do we conform to the will of the
> Almighty. The more insight we have into the will of the Almighty
> the greater will be our successes. . . .
>
> We shape the life of our people and our legislation according to
> the verdicts of genetics.[23]

No cross here, but a success story! No suffering servanthood
here, but rather a vulgar social Darwinism.

The logic of *Mein Kampf* is theological,[24] and the central
Antisemitism of nazism was far more revealing than ordinary
race prejudice. What was at work in Christendom, in the heartland of the Reformation, was an ideology, a system, and ultimately a government which was in final rebellion against the
Jewishness of holy history, against the God of the Bible, and
against the people who signalized a system of being with which
nazism was incompatible. The fact that the professors who tried
so desperately to blend Christianity with nazism were fooled by
individuals more cunning than they is really irrelevant. The
importance of their statements and actions is that they show
how generally indiscipline and heresy had penetrated the
churches.

In *Politisches Christentum* (1935), Paul Althaus greeted
Adolf Hitler as the promised *Wundermann*, like Alexander the
Great an historical appearance who stands above the laws. In
Die Herrschaft Christi und die Herrschaft von Menschen
(1936), Werner Elert declared that a Christian always obeys the
established authorities. As late as 1966 a third Erlangen Lutheran professor, Emanuel Hirsch, declared in *Ethos und Evan-
gelium* that the work of the gospel is to deepen the existing
human ethos. Examples of the philosophy of accommodation
could be listed almost indefinitely, examples of the way in

which a relativized and emasculated "Christian" faith was put forward by churchmen. But the practice of promoting culture-religion and rejecting biblical counterculture did not begin at Erlangen, or in the Third Reich; it was well advanced and articulate during the German national revival following the Napoleonic wars.

Friedrich D. E. Schleiermacher, prestigious Berlin preacher and teacher, wrote in the early nineteenth century that "Christianity stands, of course, in a special historical connection with Judaism, but as far as its historical existence and its aim are concerned, it is related to Judaism and paganism in the same way." This error, repeated hundreds of times in liberal Protestantism, has been dissected by a Danish Lutheran theologian, Kristen E. Skydsgaard, in a publication of the Lutheran World Federation. Professor Skydsgaard, thoroughly grounded in the theological and practical lessons of the Church Struggle with nazism, puts the matter this way:

> Schleiermacher's view is posited on a fundamental misunderstanding of the relationship between Judaism and Christianity, a misunderstanding that has more than once been fatal for Protestant theology since Schleiermacher. Instead of seeing the relationship in terms of *Heilsgeschichte*, it is seen in terms of the psychology of religion. Forgotten was the fact that the God who spoke to and dealt with his people was the God and the father of Jesus Christ.
>
> The fact was also overlooked that Israel continues to be the people of God, that God does not forget, even though his hand may be heavy upon them. Israel's life through the centuries and its continuing existence today is, in fact, a witness to God's hidden ways with his people.[25]

In short, Schleiermacher's bent toward general abstractions and universal principles made him forget the central story.

In the same volume a German Lutheran theologian shows how the historical perspectives have changed among those Christians who have begun to master the lessons of the Church Struggle and the Holocaust:

> In the midst of the Christian West millions of Jews fell victim to a senseless and absurd post-Christian ideology; and in the midst of a

secularized world as a fruit of Zionism there has arisen in the "Holy Land" a State of Israel which is being reconstructed by Jews from all over the world, united by the language of the Bible. While this establishes for Israel a bit of earthly homeland, Christians are to a large extent being thrust back into their true and proper existence as "exiles of the dispersion" and "aliens" (I Peter 1:1, 2:11). They are learning what the Goluth has meant for the Jews through centuries.[26]

With what reluctance, however, do the churches encounter this reversal of roles! How fond they are of establishment, how suspicious they are of pilgrimage! And how vehemently do many churchmen defend "Christendom," for which there is no New Testament justification, while they attack "Ziondom" (that is, the state of Israel, for which the Bible provides whole chapters of affirmation)! "Oh, how heavy is the weight of nineteenth-century theological Liberalism upon us still!"[27]

In America, the last major intact bloc of nineteenth-century culture-religion still resists the call to counterculture and heartily affirms "the American way of life" (or sometimes "the Southern way of life"). And, although active political Antisemitism is largely confined to the Christian underworld, an endemic cultural Antisemitism weighs heavily upon the churches. The record of the *Christian Century,* the leading liberal Protestant journal, documents the point fully.[28] Over decades, and under every editor but Kyle Haselden and James Wall (the present incumbent), a veritable flood of editorials and articles has repeated all of the traditional cultural-Antisemitic[29] charges and demands against "the Jews":

> the Jews must assimilate and become loyal members of American democratic society (9 June 1937, p. 735);
> the Jews are warned that they cannot be protected from the consequences if they stubbornly insist on being different and separate (9 June 1937, p. 735);
> international Jewish agencies are said to operate "outside the law of nations" (25 June 1947, p. 789);
> Jewish "nationalism" was comparable to German nationalism, being based on the fallacy of "a privileged race" (9 June 1937, p. 736);
> the Jews are responsible for Antisemitism because of their "social

unassimilability" (24 September 1941, pp. 1167–69);

during the Third Reich, Jewish immigration to Palestine *and* to the USA (even on temporary visas) was opposed (30 November 1938, pp. 1456–58);

American Jews were charged with slighting America's interests by promoting action against Hitler (18 June 1941, pp. 796–97);

the Jews were charged with false propaganda in reporting the Holocaust (9 December 1942, pp. 1518–19);

help was urged for *Christian* refugees (including converted Jews) fleeing Nazi-controlled Europe, but not for Jews (1 March 1939, pp. 270–72);

Christian churchmen favoring the opening of Palestine to Jewish refugees from Hitler's Europe were attacked (20 December 1936, pp. 1, 41–43);

the Jews should add Christian materials to their synagogue worship (20 December 1939, pp. 1566–67);

President Truman's recognition of Israel was due to the Jewish vote in New York City[30] (12 March 1947, p. 323; 26 May 1948, p. 500);

Israel is too much influenced by excessive Jewish orthodoxy (28 February 1951, p. 260);

Israel is a state without God (9 June 1948, p. 565).

And so on. Some of these criticisms of "the Jews" sound political rather than heretical; but they, and the editorial policy that featured them, derive uniformly from an unreflective cultural Antisemitism.

A review published in 1968 shows that neither the *Christian Century* nor liberal Protestantism generally has yet recognized the time of its visitation, and it can stand as a symbol of the continuing problem. The book was Arthur Hertzberg's *The French Enlightenment and the Jews* (1968), and the reviewer demanded that the Jews give up their separation and assimilate: "If this raises special problems in Judaism, the rest of us have also had to put aside ancestral traditions."[31] Precisely! To have faith is to remember, to recapitulate, to reenact. And the children of the Enlightenment—having abandoned any old-fashioned notions of the church as an "elect" or "separate" people, having gone over from the biblical view that history is carried by a chosen people to a general notion of social progress— cannot possibly understand the mystery of Jewish particularism and universalism. They think that the problem is "the Jews," but the real problem is that they—baptized and abstractly Christian—have long since forgotten what a pilgrim church, a faithful people, is. Their heresy is less obvious than that of "Christian" movements and spokesmen in an advanced state of disintegration, for example, the "Aryan Christians" whom Bonhoeffer sought unsuccessfully to have condemned as heretical at the Faith and Order meeting in Fanø, Denmark (1934). But they are far more dangerous, for their slurring of the issues and the dignity of their ecclesiastical positions lead the Christian constituencies as a whole to accept teachings and countenance actions which are not only sub-Christian but anti-Christian.

Apostasy

Heresy is teaching which claims to be Christian but is in fact contrary to biblical standards. *Apostasy* is the abandonment of loyalty to a community and its beliefs. In the Third Reich the slide into "Aryan" decrees and mass murder by Protestants and Roman Catholics was accepted by most adherents to Christianity. Preparation for the decline had been made by generations during which to think Christianly and to act accordingly had become confused, ambiguous concepts. The harvest of mass apostasy had been seeded by an essentially frivolous attitude to Christian teaching and discipline on the part of persons who broke their vows to "uphold the form of sound words and doctrine." It is true that each must finally answer personally for the condition of his own conscience. It is also true that when the flock drifts far astray and wanders into mortal danger the shepherds are uniquely guilty.

Was "the teaching of contempt" (Jules Isaac) "heretical"? However much we may today think it wrong, however strongly ecumenical councils and synods have subsequently spoken out, we Christians cannot claim that forty years ago the teaching of contempt was heretical. The most respected church fathers and the most authoritative synods had for centuries taught lies about the Jewish people and approved cruel and inhuman treatment of Jews. But such were wrong also before the Spirit of Truth had led the churches to correct some points in their Antisemitism. The errors, sins, and guilt of Christendom cannot be denied truthfully. But during the Third Reich the teachings and practices went far beyond the theological Antisemitism of the educated and the cultural Antisemitism of both the educated and the masses of Christians. The definition of an "Aryan" Christianity was heretical. The establishment of "Aryan" congregations was heretical. Deference to political authority rather than obedience to the (admittedly imperfect) creeds and confessions was heretical.

To press the point, important as it is: war and the conduct of war have in recent times been condemned by church councils, but there is as yet no consensus as to when and where and under what circumstances the Christians must become conscientious objectors. Participation in war and the evils attendant on it cannot yet be termed heretical conduct. But justifying atrocities, justifying the killing of defective persons and the murder of socially or racially defined groups, is—even in a national emergency—heretical for Christians. Since the Nuremberg and Tokyo Trials of Major War Criminals, and especially since the Convention of 1948, genocide has been a defined crime. Before that it was wrong, but it was not a crime. But excusing genocide, writing or speaking in support of it, was already, for Christians, heretical.

The problem was, and in most of Christendom yet remains, that under pressure and temptation most of the church leaders and the masses of the baptized will allow their thought and action to be controlled by the demands of "patriotism" and the nation-state rather than hold the line even where the churches have drawn it. And since governments of the modern type, including totalitarian states, rest upon a popular consensus, conflicts of loyalties arise which never existed in earlier centuries. Under earlier tribal dynasties, under kings who ruled "by divine right," no conflict of conscience arose for the ordinary Christian. The decisions were hammered out by the rulers of church and state, and the Christian's duty was loyal obedience. Today, since he participates to some degree in the political process and increasingly in the decision-making of the churches, the layman is confronted from time to time by a conflict of collective opinions. Most commonly, the political collective justifies measures which are in principle—and sometimes explicitly—contrary to the *consensus fidelium*. And in such a season, few indeed held to the higher loyalty. The vast majority will follow the orders of the nation-state and be thankful that there is an ample supply of false prophets to tell them that to do so is also to obey the gods.

The characteristic marks of the modern age of Christendom are, therefore, the rise of totalitarian ("post-Christian") ideologies; the mass apostasy of the gentiles ("Christians"); a sharp conflict between political rulers and that minority of baptized gentiles which strives to maintain a minimum Christian standard of conduct ("the Church Struggle"), with the political rulers supported by false prophets; the slaughter of those who by their very existence—and regardless of their personal opinions —signal the falsehood of the totalitarian visions, heroes, and history ("the Holocaust"). An uneasy peace between the superhuman state and the baptized is possible, on the other hand, because most of the Christians will obey men rather than God, will apostatize. And when the "Christians" show their true colors and go over to the Adversary, the Jews are left exposed as the one continuing counterculture which cannot assimilate, which cannot become good gentile heathen again.

Conditioned to flee from history, to avoid confrontation if at all possible, enlightened Christians have long preferred a spiritualized "Judaism" to having to deal with the Jewish people. The Christians have long since spiritualized "Christianity" and the Christian church to the point where few if any primary outward signs remain of what was once called to be "a peculiar people . . . Which in time past were not a people, but are now the people of God" (1 Peter 2:9–10). The advantage of a spiritualized, ethereal "church" is that adherents are then relieved of the burden of maintaining a counterculture; they can identify wholeheartedly with the prevailing social values, whatever they may be at a given time and place. That the Christian church has made great contributions in areas where old social orders are in dissolution—as in the tribal chaos of the Middle

Ages or in the recent collapse of tribalism and animism in Africa
—is not disputed. But, with few exceptions, the churches have
taken the path of accommodation and acculturation where confronted by powerful, intact social structures and value systems.
And they have joined in the general resentment of the Jews,
indeed blessed it, for persisting as a separate people and not
assimilating too.

Culture-Christianity greatly prefers Jews who assimilate to
Jews who remain Jews, precisely because Jews who persist in
maintaining a counterculture are an unpleasant reminder that
New Testament standards require Christians to be a counterculture too, separate from the age that is passing away. The
contemporary gentile demand upon the Jews to settle for "Judaism" has been rightly dissected by a German scholar:

> The treatment of the Jewish *people* as "religion" is in the verbal
> sense the spiritual murder of a "people," genocide. The real connec-
> tion between spiritualizing–pseudo-scientific theory and the prac-
> tice of the murder of a "people" can be perceived readily enough.
> Only this time the theologians cannot hide themselves, as in the case
> of the Nazi genocide, behind the secularistic activists: This time they
> are quite directly involved with the poetential murderers.
>
> Now as earlier the people is spiritualized down to "a religion," and
> thus this Christian spiritualizing has long served as a dependable
> instrument of Arab and European-American political propaganda
> by leftist intellectuals against Israel.[32]

Both Jews and Christians should know now that the Jewish
people cannot blend, assimilate, and disappear into some gentile society or other, although in societies whose thought-struc-
tures are dominated by the Enlightenment (such as the USA
and the USSR) individual Jews can do so. Even then it usually
takes two or three generations for Jews to disengage from a
tradition that goes back more than a hundred generations. In
"enlightened" areas, all a Jew has to do to be homogenized is
to cease to participate in the life of Israel. But when the violent
and "post-Christian" systems emerge, even that option may be
denied him; the determination to destroy a people and what
they represent becomes a huge vacuum cleaner that sweeps up

even individual Jews who have become Antisemitic renegades, or converts to Christianity, or individualistic secular humanists. In the Third Reich, the Adversary demonstrated that Jewish peoplehood is neither "a religion" nor a "spiritual" concept; it is a concrete, specific, historical fact and force.

In the French Revolutionary Assembly, Clermont-Tonnerre pronounced the "line" which has dominated "enlightened" thinking ever since: "We must refuse everything to the Jews as a Nation, but must grant the Jews everything as individuals."[33] From Napoleon Bonaparte to Arnold J. Toynbee, from Hegel to Charles Clayton Morrison, this has been the cornerstone of modern cultural Antisemitism, just as the superseding myth is the cornerstone of theological Antisemitism. Both the "enlightened" intellectual line and the traditional theological line carry the genocidal message. In liberal Protestantism, with its combination of a residue of Christian teaching and enlightened individualism, both principles are at work: the Jew must convert, or in any case he must disappear. If he remains loyal to his fathers and fathers' fathers, if he stubbornly maintains in some fashion—and however loosely!—his relationship to the Jewish people, he is resented. But that resentment arises from an unsound political premise, combined with a false religious teaching. The Jews have been chosen, as the Christians have been called, to be "a people." And a just government, one that respects human liberty and dignity, will protect the rights and liberties of dissonant communities as well as dissenting individuals.

The meaning of the Holocaust for Christians is at least this: when the baptized betray their baptism, when those who have been grafted into history flee back out of history, when the "new men" and "new women" in Christ cast off the new life and become part of the dying age again, the "old Israel" is left alone as the sign that the God who is God yet rules and that— in spite of all world conquerers and posturing false prophets— his Kingdom shall triumph in the end. *For Christians only:* We must begin our agonizing self-assessment and reappraisal with the fact that in a season of betrayal and faithlessness the vast majority of the martyrs for the Lord of history were Jews. The

Jewish people carried history while the Christians fled headlong from their professed vocation.

The time of testing ended in death for six million Jews and apostasy by uncounted millions of Christians. The critical factor was the same in both cases: *peoplehood.* The Jews died because they were standing alone and not numbered among the nations of the earth. The Christians, with the exception of a minority of martyrs and confessors, betrayed the life into which they were called.

NOTES

1. Richard L. Rubenstein, "Some Perspectives on Religious Faith after Auschwitz," in *The German Church Struggle and the Holocaust,* ed. Franklin H. Littell and Hubert G. Locke (Detroit: Wayne State University Press, 1974), pp. 260–62. For a fuller exposition of Rubenstein's theological reflections see *After Auschwitz* (New York: Bobbs-Merrill Co., 1966).

2. Martin Buber, *Tales of the Hassidim: the Early Masters* (New York: Schocken Books, 1968), p. 4.

3. Johan M. Snoek, *The Grey Book* (New York: Humanities Press, 1970), p. 292.

4. Ariah L. Bauminger, *Roll of Honour* (Tel Aviv: "Hamanova" Publishing House, 1971), p. 38.

5. Willem A. Visser't Hooft, *Die Welt war meine Gemeinde* (Munich: R. Piper & Co., 1972), p. 500.

6. Cf. Appendix A, p. 000.

7. Address: Deposit, New York 13754.

8. Address: c/o National Conference of Christians and Jews, 43 West 57th Street, New York City 10019. For a review of these developments, see Franklin H. Littell, "Recent Jewish History: Lessons for Christians," in *Gratz College Annual,* 1 (Philadelphia, 1972), pp. 107–19.

9. Karl Barth, *Verheissung und Verantwortung der Christlichen Gemeinde im Leutigen Zeitgeschehen* (Zurich: Evang. Verlag, 1944), p. 16.

10. Karl Barth, *The Church and the Political Problem of Our Day* (New York: Charles Scribner's Sons, 1939), p. 51.

11. Bishop Mugavero, in *Brothers in Hope,* ed. John M. Oesterreicher (New York: Herder & Herder, 1970), p. 254. Apart from the most important question, raised in the text of this writing, the statement also misunderstands the nature of "secularism" and "secularization"; cf. Franklin H. Littell, "The Secular City and Christian Self-Restraint," in *The Church and the Body Politic* (New York: Seabury Press, 1969), ch. 6. Further, the communities of faith have not been battered from outside by unbelievers; they have been battered by renegades and apostates, usually as much at home inside as outside.

12. Karl Kupisch, "Wider die Ächtung der Geschichte," in *Wider die Äch-*

tung der Geschichte, ed. Kurt Töpner (Munich: Bechtle Verlag, 1969), pp. 107–28.

13. Carl J. Friedrich, "Israel and the End of History," in *Israel: Its Role in Civilization,* ed. Moshe Davis (New York: Harper & Bros., 1956), p. 96.

14. Emil L. Fackenheim, "Jewish Faith and the Holocaust," *Commentary* (August 1968), vol. 46, pp. 30–36. "A Jew may not respond to Hitler's attempt to destroy Judaism by himself cooperating in its destruction."

15. Eric Voegelin, *The New Science of Politics* (Chicago: University of Chicago Press, 1952), p. 9.

16. Ibid., pp. 131, 132.

17. Eric Voegelin, *Order and History, I: Israel and Revelation* (Baton Rouge: Louisiana State University Press, 1956), pp. 120 f.

18. Cited in John S. Conway, *The Nazi Persecution of the Churches* (New York: Basic Books, 1968), p. 147.

19. Hans Buchheim, *Glaubenskrise im Dritten Reich* (Stuttgart: Deutsche Verlags-Anstalt, 1953), passim.

20. Helmut Heiber, ed., *The Early Goebbels Diaries* (New York: Frederick A. Praeger, 1963), p. 101.

21. Cited in Arthur C. Cochrane, *The Church's Confession under Hitler* (Philadelphia: Westminster Press, 1962), p. 183.

22. Hermann Rauschning's books document how early and explicit was Hitler's contempt for Christianity, even though he continued to deceive and confuse the pious by his public posture. Cf. *The Revolution of Nihilism* (New York: Alliance Book Corp., 1939), pp. 118–19; *The Voice of Destruction* (New York: G. P. Putnam's Sons, 1940), ch. 4. Bormann's plan for the Warthegau, personally approved by Hitler, programmed the privatization of Christianity and its eventual disappearance; Paul Gürtler, *Nationalsozialismus und evangelische Kirchen im Warthegau* (Göttingen: Vandenhoeck & Ruprecht, 1958).

23. Cited in Hannah Arendt, *The Origins of Totalitarianism* (New York: Meridian Books, 1958), pp. 346, 350. A popular SA song, which would lose its impact if translated, ran as follows:

> *Papst und rabbi sollen weiden,*
> *Heiden woll'n wir wieder sein,*
> *Nicht mehr in die Kirche schleichen,*
> *Sonnenrad führt uns allein!*

In the revolt of the heathen gods with Nazi encouragement, Mithras received his due along with Wotan, Thor, Dionysius, Apollo, and Moloch! (The writer is grateful to Msgr. John M. Oesterreicher for this item.)

24. Michael D. Ryan, "Hitler's Challenge to the Churches: A Theological Political Analysis of *Mein Kampf,*" in *The German Church Struggle and the Holocaust,* p. 152 f.

25. K. E. Skydsgaard, "Israel, the Church and the Unity of the People of God," reprint from 10 *Lutheran World* (1963) 4 and 11 *Lutheran World* (1964) 3, pp. 2, 3.

26. Leonhard Goppelt, "Israel and the Church in Today's Discussion and in Paul," ibid., p. 8.

27. Barth, *The Church and the Political Problem of Our Day*, p. 83.

28. Hertzel Fishman, *American Protestantism and the Jewish State* (Detroit: Wayne State University Press, 1973), passim.

29. The distinction between theological, cultural, and political Antisemitism is of fundamental importance. Theological Antisemitism developed in the church fathers along with the victory of Hellenistic thought and Roman law. Cultural Antisemitism was built into the language and images and instincts over centuries of "Christendom." Political Antisemitism is an ideological weapon, used by modern despotisms and totalitarian movements and regimes. A basic error of many studies of Antisemitism is that they confine use of the term to active and willful manifestations of the modern type, whereas the hidden, most deeply rooted and most dangerous sources of the evil are theological and/or cultural. See Franklin H. Littell, 1973 Israel Goldstein Lecture at Hebrew University, "Christendom, Holocaust and Israel: The importance for Christians of Recent Major Events in Jewish History," *Journal of Ecumenical Studies* (1973) 3:483–97.

30. After leaving the presidency, Harry Truman was awarded an honorary degree at Jewish Theological Seminary. The man who introduced him referred to him as a man who had contributed much to the birth of Israel. Mr. Truman responded: " '. . . a man who contributed much'? I am Cyrus. I am Cyrus!" God bless the Southern Baptist Sunday school that trained Harry Truman as a boy!

31. *Christian Century*, 28 October 1968, p. 253.

32. Friedrich-Wilhelm Marquardt, "Gottes Bundestreue und die biblischen Landverheissungen," in *Jüdische Hoffnungskraft und christlicher Glaube*, ed. Walter Strolz (Freiburg/Br.: Herder Verlag, 1971), pp. 129–30.

33. Quoted in H. G. Adler, *The Jews in Germany: From the Enlightenment to National Socialism* (Notre Dame: University of Notre Dame Press, 1969), p. 3.

V

ISRAEL: THE CRISIS OF CHRISTIANITY

In his analysis of the encounter of the Arab world with Israel, Johan Bouman has concluded:

> Israel represents—whether it wishes to or not—the crisis of Islam. Whether this crisis can be resolved is still an open question, and until then the unrest of the Arab-Islamic world will be directed toward Israel. For what is here at stake is the justification of the identity not only of a people, but a religion and a culture, which for centuries played a leading part in the earth. . . . As a foreign body, Israel has brought out a sense of fundamental insecurity.[1]

In a sense the crisis in Islam is deeper than that in Christendom, for there the spiritual and intellectual unity of a prescientific religious culture has not yet entered the historical period of voluntary adherence, pluralism, skeptical study. Islam is today comparable in its monistic mindset to Christendom in the thirteenth century.

The crisis for Christendom also runs very deep, however, for the "post-Christian" systems of being—Marxism, secular humanism, positivism, various types of Fascist belief and action—must be added to the value crisis of the West. And the self-assurance of a vital oral tradition is much more seriously eroded in the "Christian" nations than in Muslim states. Even Turkey, the only country with a Muslim culture to have attempted modern politics and education, still has a great number of *hafiz* (living libraries, persons who have memorized large blocs of the sacred tradition) and a rich heritage of relatively intact common memories. In Christendom this foundation of a common culture is seriously eroded. Moreover, if the tendency in the Muslim states is toward excessive zeal and ideological crusades, the erosion of belief in Christendom has produced a cynical relativism, an "evenhandedness" between right and wrong.

During the Yom Kippur War, in which for some days the very existence of Israel was overcast with shadows, Great Britain played an "evenhanded" politics reminiscent of her "nonintervention" during the Spanish Civil War: public expressions of Antisemitic vulgarity (over BBC, in the newspapers, and even in parliament) surged to the surface; the government refused to condemn the surprise attack by Egypt and Syria; the government refused landing privileges for planes carrying emergency equipment to Israel when the arms reserve was exhausted; the government refused to ship machine parts to Israel that had been purchased and paid for; the government continued to train Egyptian pilots during the fighting. This was obviously not the same Britain that had stood courageously alone against Nazi aggression, not the same Britain even that under Anthony Eden's leadership (in May, 1967) had acted to check Nasser's illegal military actions in the Sinai and Sharm-el-Sheik, the Suez Canal, and the Straits of Tiran.

France's "evenhandedness" was more to be expected, perhaps, since the country has not yet dealt surgically with its own record of collaboration with the Nazis—especially in the murder of the Jews. Her government had already established itself as a dishonest broker, refusing delivery to Israel of equipment already paid for. Between the long-standing and yet unrepentant Antisemitism of the radical Right and the anti-Jewish and anti-Israel cadres of the radical Left, France had virtually no political strength left in a middle ground where nonideological decisions fair to Israel might be hammered out. France's "nonintervention" during the Yom Kippur War was signalized by continued training of Arab pilots, a surge of Antisemitic public utterance from the Gaullist right, continued arms shipments to Libya and Saudi Arabia, and so forth. The French Catholic community has a long record of Antisemitism, although some members of the hierarchy have had admirable records; the alliance of many French Protestants with "the Third World," arising in part from the Algerian struggle, has now borne fruit in bitterly Antisemitic statements and actions. During the Yom Kippur War the most hostile statements from the whole French left wing came from *Témoignage Chrétien.*

Dignity seemed best maintained by smaller and less prideful powers, as also later when the Common Market countries collapsed so pitifully in the face of blackmail by Arab oil shippers. Of the "Christian" countries under Nazi control in 1940–45, Denmark gave the single example of national Christian action. The Danes, from King Christian to the general populace, resisted the Aryan laws and by courageous action saved most Danish Jews. In recent attacks on the Jews, only the Dutch government attempted a resistance of courage and honor.

Most disappointing of all was the conduct of the German *Bundesrepublik.* Disappointment arose from the fact that since 1952 the West German government has pursued an admirable policy of compensation and friendship to Israel, and something better than capitulation to Arab League pressures was to be expected. The Bonn republic's honorable restitution policy has not been matched, incidentally, by comparable acts of atonement by Austria or Communist East Germany. We now know that the collapse of Bonn to pressure may have had more sinister and specific cause than then realized, for the discovery of a high Communist agent in the chancellor's office has again demonstrated how extensive and effective has been fifth-column penetration of *Bundesrepublik* decision-making. In any case, although a *Demoskopie* survey showed 57 percent of the public pre-Israel and only 8 percent pro-Arab League, government policy was weak and equivocating. The most effective anti-Jewish force in postwar West Germany has not been residual Nazi influence; it has derived from the influence of Marxist cadres in the universities and among intellectuals. One of the tragedies of contemporary West Germany is that its youth and students are living through theoretical and practical political issues that were resolved in 1936–40 in England and the United

States, when Germany was cut off from the intellectual currents of the day.

The point is that leading "Christian" nations, once the heartland of Christendom, acted in a crucial moment without regard to religious or ethical considerations. In France the capitulation came with radical Right preference for Hitler over Leon Blum (1936); in Britain the capitulation came with radical Left sabotage of Eden's last and final action as leader of a world-minded empire (1967); in West Germany the capitulation came with radical Left sabotage of long-range and honorable commitments to Israel's survival (1973). In each case, as in other countries claiming to be "Christian" but in fact strictly self-seeking, "Christian" standards and "Christian" commitments proved to be easily sloughed off. As in many other areas, theological as well as political, the question naturally arises whether the claim to be "Christian" is anything but a sham, whether "Christendom" itself is anything but a fraud.

Here again, for the person who believes in the importance of conscious personal decision, who rejects the coercive use of state power in matters of conscience, who denies that the true church is in any sense defined by secular state authority, who denies that the proper functions of government are in any sense to be ideologically or religiously controlled, the answer to the riddle is plain. The "Christian" nations are not Christian entities at all. It is a mistake to think that they will act, when push comes to shove, from Christian presuppositions. They are in fact gentiles, and they will act accordingly; toward the Jewish people they will swing from persecution to toleration to genocide to occasional—and utterly arbitrary and fortuitous—friendliness.

It is imperative that the Christians, therefore, distinguish carefully between their expectations of the church and their expectations of civil government. In redefining the relationship of the Christian church to the Jewish people, it is more than probable that the Christians and the gentiles will move in quite different directions. One major reason why the civil society and civil government cannot today be allowed to cloak itself in the mantle of Christianity is precisely because—having misunderstood itself and its function—such government easily swings tomorrow to a post-Christian ideology of Marxist or Fascist type. Antisemitism and oppression of the Jews has been a long-standing mark of sacral government; so is corruption of Christianity, although the baptized gentiles are often too blinded to perceive it.

We return to the crisis of Christendom: that behind the facade of official religion and state-churches there is a baptized heathenism proved capable of the most wicked rebellion against God and most murderous action against those whose very existence reminds the rebellious gentiles of him.

The Free Churches

If the established churches' response to Israel's critical situation is controlled by national and ideological interests rather than Christian compassion and rectitude, what of the Free churches?

Here we enter a field of particular difficulty, for many "free churches" have in fact accepted social status and establishment even though they cling to "separation of church and state." The Virginia Bill of Religious Freedom (1784–86) and the First Amendment to the U.S. Constitution which followed upon it (1789–91) provide to be sure a separation of the religious from the political covenants. But not seldom those churches which were originally committed to voluntary membership and discipline have slipped into a style of culture-religion very little different from that of legal establishments. And when they do so, the endemic Antisemitism of the baptized gentiles surges to the surface.

A good illustration of the problem is the Quaker report entitled *Search for Peace in the Middle East*, a report which has appeared in differing editions. The Quakers are noted for— among other things—ethical sensitivity, for courage to confront unjust rulers, and for producing fruits of Christian service far beyond the natural energy of their small numbers. Yet the initial edition (May, 1970) of the report was faulted, and justly, by both Jews and Christians for being blind to basic facts about the Middle East problem. Most significant, the report ignored the fact that the Middle East conflict had produced Jewish refugees as well as Arab refugees. From all the evidence, the Quaker working party simply forgot the hundreds of thousands of Jewish refugees as they built up a case harshly critical of Israel in the name of Arab refugees.[2] And the meaning of the fact that almost all Israelis are refugees or the descendants of refugees from Christendom and Islam escaped them entirely, although the central argument of the report was humanitarian. How could this happen? It happened, and happens regularly among well-meaning liberal churchmen, because Christians are subconsciously accustomed to accept as normal the misery of Jews. Men of the Free churches, like men of the legally established churches, are riddled with ancient anti-Jewish prejudices which they have not even acknowledged—let alone repented of.

Some Free churches of Pietist heritage embraced "Key '73" as a special opportunity to missionize the Jews, without apparently ever asking themselves whether Hebrew missions can carry credibility after the action and inaction of Christians in the Holocaust. They ignored too the serious question whether there is any biblical basis for the assumption that individual Jews must convert in order to satisfy the New Testament vision of the end and fulfillment of holy history. There is in fact no passage that can be cited to justify the notion that baptized gentiles must convert Jews for the latter to be saved.[3] In the Bible, the plan of salvation expands outward from a Jewish base; it does not contract away from that center, nor does the Bible present a brand new center. The displacement theory was a gentile invention, post biblical.

In one of his great sermons Reinhold Niebuhr put the matter succinctly: ". . . It is not our business to convert Jews to Christianity. It is more important that each individual make the most creative use of the framework of meaning that each faith constructs for the faithful. . . . Let Christians be concerned with their own problems."[4] Individual conversionism directed toward the Jews is primarily a result of Pietism in the churches and the influence of the Enlightenment in philosophical circles. It was the glory of modern missions, to which Pietism contributed so much, to stress the importance of every individual soul and its own choice regardless of political or social status; it was the error of Pietism to treat the Jews as individuals only, in the same sense as Hottentots, Hurons, or Saxons.

A wise Jewish observer, Trude Weiss-Rosmarin, can explain the situation with charity:

> Naturally, "Key 1973" will also address itself to Jews—just as during an election campaign Democrats will address themselves to Republicans and Republicans will try to proselytize Democrats. This is the essence of democracy. . . . If people feel threatened by the zeal of those who "evangelize," they should intensify their own efforts and proclaim their own truth-and-message.[5]

A Christian thinker must, however, ask himself whether such individual soul-trapping of Jews can be justified at all according to the New Testament and whether it represents anything but bad faith after the Holocaust.

Men of the Free churches began to go astray on the Christian relationship to the Jewish people quite early—in the sixteenth century, in fact, long before either Pietism or the Holocaust. Balthasar Hübmaier, who became an Anabaptist leader, led popular riots against the Jews in Regensburg, and the mob burned a synagogue. Menno Simons wrote extensively of the "bad" God of the Old Testament, with his wars and violence and dead laws, and contrasted him with the beautiful and loving Jesus of the Christian dispensation. In this he followed Luther. Both Menno and Luther were more superficial in their understanding of the Old Testament than reformers such as Calvin and Butzer, who took the Abrahamic covenant seriously. The point is that the left wing of the Reformation tended so to stress the "model" of the early church that it has often neglected the "model" of the Jewish people, to glory in the new covenant in Christ so greatly that it has forgotten that there were servants of the truth of God before Jesus of Nazareth and the Christian church appeared on earth. This is the road to what Dietrich Bonhoeffer rightly called "cheap grace," to a shallow Christianity which—using traditional language—misunderstands and misinterprets both the Law and the Gospel because it does not perceive how indispensable each is to the other.

Sectarian Protestantism brought a great blessing to Christianity in stressing the thought and style of life of a Christian counterculture. It also weakened Christianity seriously where that counterculture was cut off from its Jewish antecedents and alienated from the genuine model of biblical counterculture—the continuing Jewish people. Menno and other radical Protestant teachers identified a "dead" Judaism with the "dead" legalism of the religious establishments (both Roman Catholic and Protestant) that they were seceding from. What they failed to perceive was the fact that the continuing Jewish people had no more in common with Christendom than they had themselves, and that the Jews were still—as in the biblical view—an effective "model" for what a Christian counterculture should in many respects be like.

A Visible Community

In the sixteenth century the Jews were called "materialistic" for the same reason that the radical Protestants were called "monkish" and "legalistic," that is, because they believed that the faithful life carried certain definite marks and signs. As against those who spiritualized the heavenly church, removing the spiritual life from any "merely human" inventions or controls, the radical Protestants—like the Jews—believed the Scriptures gave clear indications as to what the community of the faithful looked like and acted like. Against the notion of a purely "invisible church," known only to God, so completely split from the earthly church that the latter can compromise and accommodate to any political power, social control, or ecclesiastical pattern, both Anabaptists and Jews affirmed that the true and faithful community is a counterculture. In vital religion, the faith is never a mere creature of the dominant culture; on the contrary, the culture is shaped by the faith.

There are events in the present life of the Jewish community from which Christians can learn with great benefit. This is especially true today when the Jewish counterculture is undergoing a tremendous spiritual and cultural and intellectual renewal, whereas much Christian congregational life is dull in worship and in culture is virtually indistinguishable from the Rotarians or the country club. Assuming that Christianity may be renewed too, that the Christian people will work their way through the lessons of the Holocaust and a restored Israel to a reformed teaching and recovered credibility, certain specific lessons will be noted. The Christians may learn and appropriate not only from the life of the Jews of old but from the continuing community of Jewish faithful.

In the annual liturgical calendar. In the patristic period the close connection of Christian and Jewish festivals was deliberately broken by the gentiles. Most conspicuously, the Christians began to observe Sunday rather than the Sabbath. And Easter (which the earliest Christians considered "the Christian Passover") was put on a different schedule from Passover (Pesach). Among Jewish liturgical events of great spiritual vitality, the Passover Seder is especially adaptable to Christian family use.

The Jewish community has retained far better than most Christians the vitality of family observance and worship. Probably among Christians the Christmas Eve services best continue some remnants of family worship—with recitation, singing, and prayer; but here the tendency in recent decades has been for special congregational services to move into whatever space is left when a tawdry commercialism has squeezed the spirit dry. But the Passover Seder[6] celebrates an event which has primordial significance for Christian as well as Jewish faith: the deliverance out of slavery in Egypt. A significant number of readings and prayers link the Exodus with continuing efforts to attain full liberty and dignity for all mankind. The scriptural passages and prayers are evocative and meaningful for believing Christians as well as for Jews. Parts of the service are especially intended for children's participation, which is important for a full family festival. Certain foods, special dishes, and baked goods are peculiar to the occasion; American gentile mothers who have in recent decades developed skill in Mexican, Chinese, and even Indonesian cooking will hardly be baffled by Passover specialties—especially with Jewish neighbors who will be glad to lend recipes and advice.

The Passover Seder today includes readings and prayers

memorializing the victims of the Holocaust. Christian families will naturally include readings from the writings of Christian martyrs who perished at the hands of the same murderers; there are no finer testimonies in Christian history than can be selected from the letters of Paul Schneider, Dietrich Bonhoeffer, Helmuth von Moltke, Alfred Delp, Franz Jägerstätter.

The Christian annual calendar should also include a special service memorializing the victims of the Holocaust. Although it is spiritually perilous for anyone to "appropriate" the event, it is imperative that Christian families and congregations come to terms with its meaning. Whatever the theoretical problems, sensitive souls are coming to realize that what happened at Auschwitz must be memorialized and mastered, and not only by Jews. Now that the raw question of survival has been resolved for the Jews, the major crisis has passed from them to the Christians. The most profound disservice of Hebrew Christian missioners is precisely this: that they continue to direct attention to the traditional crisis put by Christianity to the Jewish people, whereas the central issue today is the crisis put to Christianity by a crucified and resurrected Jewry.

Let the Christian congregations and families use a service such as that prepared by Elizabeth Wright,[7] and let them read together from such a poem of faith as Elie Wiesel's *Ani Maamin*,[8] and the confronting question will inevitably arise: "Were you there when they crucified my Lord?" And beyond that comes a second question of self-appraisal for Christians: Where in Christendom is today to be found such vibrant affirmation of the debate with God, such vital confidence in the One who is sent to redeem a mankind wallowing in its own wickedness?

In the annual calendar of some churches, the Day of the Covenant was once a meaningful appropriation from the Jewish tradition. At this time the Christians remembered and reenacted their participation in God's promises to Abraham, reaffirmed to Jacob and his seed. There are still vestigial remains: in South Africa the "day" has become confused with racial memories, and the Old Testament sign is blended with the Voortrekker river crossing; among American Methodists,

John Wesley's memorialization of the divine covenant has been shallowed out to an annual pledge against use of alcohol. Once a year in the Christian congregation a Day of the Covenant is needed in which all the people repeat the vows they made upon becoming witting members of the covenant community. The liturgy of the day will stress both the common and personal dimensions of the events which created a people and grafted each person present into that history.

In the weekly liturgical calendar. In Jewish congregational worship the members of the family stand at a certain point and recite the memorial prayer on the anniversary of the death of a parent. This *Yarzeit* event is a most impressive affirmation of the truth that the fellowship of the faithful binds together the generations, transcends life and death. We Christians refer to "the communion of saints" in repeating the creed, but we tend at best to give it a horizontal dimension, stressing interracial, interdenominational, worldwide fellowship in Christ. The communion of saints becomes in this fashion a spiritual entity of those living and present. As important as this truth is, although only if incarnated in style of life and fraternal good works, without regular remembrance that the majority of the faithful are those who have died in the faith it becomes a mere will-o'-the-wisp. It is the readiness to stand squarely in a real historical tradition, the readiness to reaffirm and reenact the faith of fathers and fathers' fathers, which saves Jewish worship from the vacuous rootlessness of much of "Christian fellowship." The key sign for a vital Christianity is sacrament, not sentiment. By developing a *Yarzeit* service we can begin to recover the concreteness, the earthiness, the historical specificity from which an unformed and ethereal Christian "spirituality" has taken headlong flight.

A second occasion which may become a regular feature of the weekly service is a Christian initiation ceremony comparable to the Bar Mitzvah (or Bat Mitzvah). Although a few denominations give fairly full attention to catechetical and/ or confirmation training, which is a minimal undertaking, we lack a signal event in the life of the boy or girl passing into manhood or womanhood in the Christian congregation. In many churches,

especially in the European establishments, the class exercises
held for a group once a year are the last time the young adult
appears in the public worship of God. What is needed is a time
of personal choice and affirmation, when each consciously and
in solemn deliberation makes public profession of his own faith.

The leaders of the post-Christian creeds, Nazi and Communist, are well aware of the importance of initiation rites; they
have developed ideological confirmation events (*Jugendweihe*,
and so forth) placed in deliberate competition to Christian and
Jewish confirmations. But since their goal is sacral and social
control, they cannot feature individual decision; the state dedication ceremonies are always collective affairs. For this reason
some of the pastors of the resisting churches have called for a
Christian ceremony to be held later, after the state dedication
of the youth class, at a time of more mature personal decision,
featuring a personal affirmation rather than a massed formation.

In the Jewish congregation, at the appropriate age the young
adult participates in the public worship of God by reading from
the Scriptures and receiving the prayers and blessings of the
assembled people. There is scarcely a Christian congregation
whose liveliness and meaningfulness on a Sunday morning
would not be substantially improved by celebration of such an
event in the life of a young member. And there is no Christian
whose entrance into Christian adulthood in the church would
not be given much greater and deeper value by such an occasion.

Among those smaller churches which still retain a strictly
structured ritual of individual conversion, profession of faith,
and believer's baptism, the need for such a ritual is less. But for
most of Christendom the proposal is sound. Even those
churches which once had something comparable have cheap-
ened the event. The Southern Baptists have been riddled by
child evangelism and statistical ambition and are baptizing children into full membership. The Episcopalians have moved
confirmation (which originated in Strassburg in 1533 as an alternative to adult baptism and was brought by the exiled Martin
Butzer into the second Book of Common Prayer!) down to years
too tender to carry the real meaning of initiation with one's

peer group. The celebration of a personal event, as here proposed, will serve several purposes; most important, by conscious choice the young adult celebrates with the faithful living and dead one of the most memorable events of his own life.

The Land of Israel

For generations "enlightened" Christians have criticized the Jewish people and secretly resented them because they have resisted assimilation into the progressive gentile society. Napoleon attacked them for their stubborn and peculiar food laws, refusal to intermarry, use of Hebrew instead of French. Stalin and his successors have applied every pressure to liquidate a peculiar people. Liberal Protestants have denigrated their loyalty to "obscurantist" traditions and "irrational" mysteries. Most difficult of all has been the question of the land.

That a specific land was part of the original promises of God to his people can scarcely be disputed.[9] These pious Jews who still take the covenant seriously are accused of building an intolerant and sacral society. (Perhaps from their own history, the Christian's cannot imagine a comprehensive devotion to religion that is not intolerant!) Those modernized Jews who reject a literal interpretation of classical teachings are accused of "secularism," "lack of spirituality," even irreligion and atheism. In short, the customary double standard, bolstered by the endemic Antisemitism of Christendom, finds fault with the Jews whatever they think or do.

In point of truth, however, "Ziondom" has far better scriptural foundation than Christendom. So far as biblical teaching is concerned, Jewish peoplehood and nationhood and attachment to the land is the only kind of ethnic identity to which God has given explicit approval. When the gentile tribes move in that direction, as they in fact often have, they do so in direct opposition to the course laid out for them.

In stubborn fashion, and in spite of flirtations with assimilation at different seasons and in different places, the Jews have clung to history, earthiness, concrete events. And Israel, which came into being as part of a specific series of historical events, cannot properly be judged by persons whose dominant thought patterns are ruled by a flight from history. Whether expressed in traditional terms, in which a spiritualized and heavenly "church" was posited as balance to a thoroughly compromised and corrupted Christian religion, or expressed in the emancipated propositions and theories of post-Enlightenment Christianity, the effect is the same: Christians constantly judge Israel and Diaspora Jewry in rarified terms, in terms meaningless to Jews and irrelevant to biblical Christianity. The sword which cuts the Gordian knot is the awareness that the Jewish people has a right to self-definition and that nothing less than that affirmation is worthy of Christians.

The restitution of Israel is the event which challenges Christians to take events, history, and the world seriously again. The sterility of a "spirituality" in which nothing important happens between the Ascension and the Second Coming has been exposed to sight.

That there are Jews who have no interest in Israel or Jewish community life is not denied; there are circumcized goyim just as there are baptized heathen. But the renewal of Jewish life, the most striking theological development today, is based on an awareness of certain historical truths. First, the Adversary identifies the Jew, even if he is personally uncertain who he is. This lesson was taught by Adolf Hitler and Josef Stalin. Second, the Christian establishment cannot be counted on for humanitarian, let alone fraternal, intervention to prevent or even impede the mass murder of Jews. This lesson was taught by the heads of the Roman Catholic, Protestant, and Orthodox churches during the Holocaust itself and during subsequent threats such as the Yom Kippur War. Third, the continued existence of Israel and its social, educational, and cultural growth depend primarily upon the vitality of Israelis and the sacrifice of overseas Jewry. It is true that the shifting tides of power and superpower competition sometimes fortuitously work to Israel's advantage; far more common, in an age when all industrialized nations are easily blackmailed by those who control the sources of energy, is the isolation of Israel by Communist and Arab League blocs—supinely tolerated by Japan and Western

Europe and, not infrequently, America.

The new code word for Antisemitism is *Anti-Zionism*, whether the slogan is uttered by Communists, Arab League propagandists, adherents of the "New Left," or liberal Protestants. Theoretically, one can be tolerant of Roman Catholics and work day and night for the destruction of the papacy. Theoretically, one can be tolerant of Methodists and Baptists and forbid them interracial meetings and public dissemination of their literature. Theoretically, one can be tolerant of Hutterite views and legislate against communal holding of property. In the concrete and specific, however, such distinctions are without a difference. No one can be an enemy of Zionism and be a friend of the Jewish people today—not the czar, not the Soviets, not the *Deutsche Christen*, not the *United Church Observer.*

America and the Holy Land

One of the major disasters of American Protestantism was the elimination of the Hebrew language requirement from most seminary education. This is not the moment to discuss what the elimination of the Greek language requirement has contributed toward letting loose on the churches a clergy unable to distinguish *agape* from *eros.* But it is timely to point out that the use of the Old Testament in Sunday liturgies and preaching has declined in recent generations, and that liberal Protestantism in America—in its basic doctrines: God, church, Jesus Christ, relation to society, sacraments, culture or counterculture, understanding of tradition and confessions of faith, view of law and order, attitude to the Jewish people—is very little different from the liberal Protestantism of Germany which accommodated so readily to nazism.

Some evangelical churches have been making a strong effort to recover and reaffirm the essential Jewishness of Christianity. A sign of this is the broad student participation in the excellent program of the American Institute for Holy Land Studies conducted by Dr. G. Douglas Young in Jerusalem. An exception to the criticism of more liberal leadership should also be made for study seminars such as those conducted by Prof. Charles Fritsch of Princeton, Prof. Lionel Whiston of Eden, Prof. Robert Handy of Union (New York). Professor Handy's program of seminar and publications on America and the Holy Land, codirected with Prof. Moshe Davis of Jewish Theological Seminary and Hebrew University, is especially commendable.

As a whole, however, the American churches have not yet begun to capitalize on the potential of study in Israel as a basic part of theological education. To date organized pilgrimages are more common in the continuing education of the clergy than is experience in the Holy Land during the most impressionable and formative stage of all, the seminary years. Here again the Jewish agencies and institutions are far ahead of the Christian boards and schools. More and more young rabbis are spending at least a year in Israel, improving their use of the language and expanding their sense of the times and places where occurred the formative biblical events. One Jewish denomination now proposes to establish its major university of Judaism in Jerusalem, with its seminaries in America serving as feeder schools and all of its young rabbis studying in Israel. With travel as easy as it is today, and with tens of thousands of undergraduate students spending a summer or a year abroad, such a plan is feasible and attractive. There is no good reason why Christian seminaries should not develop a similar plan, and there is much that argues for it. Most important, no other program would so quickly reestablish the Jewish component in the preaching and teaching of the churches; no other action would move so rapidly to dispel the idle vapors of a sentimental "spirituality" and renew the consciousness of a providential history involving real persons, concrete events, and specific commitments.

The renewal of the Holy Land connection is imperative for the churches: first, to purge the false teaching that the Jewish people is dying out or losing its vital place in holy history; second, to revitalize a Christianity that has lost contact with real events and ceased to speak about them.

The crucifixion and resurrection of the Jewish people is a sign that God is not mocked, that pride brings the biggest battalions low in the end, that the Author and the Judge of history blesses the Suffering Servant and brings the human hero low. Do the baptized still believe these truths, or must they be numbered among the blind and deaf when the Messiah comes?

NOTES

1. Johan Bouwman, "Die arabische Welt angesichts Israel," 8 *Emuna* (1973) 4:258.

2. Cf. A. Roy, Eckardt, "Anti-Israelism, Antisemitism, and the Friends," in *CCI Notebook* No. 3 (June 1971).

3. Cf. "Convert the Jews?" in *CCI Notebook* No. 13 (June 1973).

4. Reinhold Niebuhr, "The Son of Man Must Suffer," in *Justice and Mercy,* ed. Ursula M. Niebuhr (New York: Harper & Row, 1974), p. 87.

5. Trude Weiss-Rosmarin, "Key 1973" in *Jewish Observer,* 3 February 1973, p. 2.

6. The Passover liturgy is available in English in two beautiful books, one Conservative and the other Reform: *The Passover Haggadah,* ed. Morris Silverman (Bridgeport, Conn.: Prayer Book Press, 1972); *A Passover Haggadah,* ed. Herbert Bronstein (New York: Central Conference of American Rabbis, 1974).

7. Appendix B.

8. Elie Wiesel, *Ani Maamin* (New York: Random House, 1973).

9. See Appendix A, paragraphs 7, 8.

VI

THE DEBATE WITH GOD

Fright before any threat of open confrontation prejudges the final encounter. In fact, the present dead state of the debate with God among the Christians was predicted by their failure to engage vigorously in the debates with and for man. The angel of the Lord with whom the devout must wrestle is "unknown," as Charles Wesley's hymn, "Come, O Thou Traveler Unknown," puts it, precisely because in that encounter the man of faith is at one moment face to face with the human countenance and at the next moment encountering the divine glory. Just as the love of God and the love of neighbor are two sides of the same coin, so the encounter with the divine can never be divided from the encounter with human persons, problems, and decisions. A series of failures in the debates which surround concrete historical decisions is predictive of failure in the highest court of all.

In the Church Struggle, the debate with the heretics was earnest enough, had the church leaders considered their task a serious one. The "Confession of Faith" of the *Deutsche Christen*, on whose behalf Hitler intervened personally in the church elections, left no ambiguity as to their ultimate commitment to the tribe, the ethnic group.

> The basic aim of all religious and church politics of the union must be the erection of the fifth pillar, the Church—however it may be named—beside the four remaining pillars of party, government,

military, industry. These are all only functions of the *Volk*. From the *Volk* they derive their justification; in their proper function they express the life of the *Volk*.[1]

Another document, the "Decalogue" of the *Deutsche Christen,* carried as point seven—"We see in race, *Volkstum* and Nation orders of life given us and entrusted to us by God; the maintenance of them is God's law."[2] This affirmation, which is, nevertheless, a perversion of Luther's teaching on the Orders of Creation, sounded pious to the masses of the baptized and also confused many of the church leaders and theologians.

Most churchmen were of course unaware of the plan of Hitler and Bormann to liquidate the Christian churches, and few had heard the judge of the People's Court (Freisler) declare to the martyr, Helmuth von Moltke, "You know, the only thing we have in common with Christianity is this: we National Socialists also demand the whole person."[3] But there was public evidence enough to require a decision of resistance. The overt Nazi ideology was plainly at odds with the Christian creeds and confessions, even if some Christians could truthfully say they didn't know of the atrocities committed on Nazi orders. Heresy and cynicism vie for first place in an official Nazi statement such as this:

> With the Germanic idea that a man lives on in his deeds and in his kinship *(Sippe),* one might be led to question the old Christian idea of life after death. In the same context we should stress the honor and loyalty of those who have given their lives for the perpetuation and strengthening of the *Volksgemeinschaft,* thus providing strength and guidance for all our people, but especially for our youth. . . . With such ideas we can satisfy the people's need for a religion in time of war.[4]

It should be unnecessary to underline the naked unbelief which rings through this official statement of policy.

The Confessing church in Germany and some judicatories in countries under Nazi occupation came off fairly well in the debate with heresy. For example, a Dutch Pastoral of 1943 stated the fundamental antagonism of the Nazi creed and system to Christianity in quite precise traditional terms:

> Nothing—we repeat, nothing—may be itself and develop according
> to its own nature, neither society nor the family nor marriage, nei-
> ther art nor the school nor the university. It is actually claimed that
> somewhere (where?) there is a gigantic superhuman intellect which
> knows everything and governs everything, which owes no one any
> explanation since it itself knows what is good and what is evil, and
> against whose decisions, judgments and actions one cannot appeal
> to any Higher Court, because ultimately there is no other court.
> There is no *ethical* reason, and there can be none, why the Church
> should not be put on the same level as everything else. . . . Within
> such a state-system it is fundamentally impossible to lead a free and
> Christian life.[5]

Nevertheless, such statements were finally inadequate to the
confrontation with heresy and unbelief. First, they carried a
serious misreading of the nature of nazism. The trouble with
nazism was not that it was secular, defending the independence
of matured institutions, but that it was intensely "spiritual" (in
a demonic sense). Part of the weakness of the churches was
precisely that they had not recognized the worth of secularized
institutions.[6] Second, and more substantial yet, was the vulnera-
bility of positions stated in strictly dogmatic and traditional
language. Wolfgang Gerlach has shown how fatal this was for
even the Confessing church, which followed Barth into dogmatic—and therefore narrowly Christian—opposition, rather
than going with Bonhoeffer into resistance on an ethical-Chris-
tian basis.[7] The dogmatic base was too narrow and did not
include in its front-line concerns the miseries and sufferings of
non-Christians.

Finally, even the narrow and traditional base was deserted by
most churchmen—and not alone in Germany. Many church
officials outside the Third Reich, in a false spirit of accommodation and harmony, opposed efforts like those of Bonhoeffer at
the Faith and Order meeting in Fanø (Denmark), 1934, to have
"Aryan" Christianity condemned as a heresy. Some, like the
Anglican bishop of Gloucester (A. C. Headlam), even intrigued
with the Nazis against the German church resistance and its
allies.[8] In Nazi-occupied France the Roman Catholic primate
(Gerlier) blessed Pétain, and the cardinal archbishop of Paris
(Beudrillant) was a regular contributor to the Nazi press. The

church took the lead in lining up youth support of the Vichy government, in collaborating with Hitler, and in March of 1942 the head of the organization of youth (1.2 million strong) declared: "Our youth are in the service of the Marshal, and they will make a more beautiful and more Christian France."[9] Eugène Cardinal Tisserant, who refused to leave Rome and visit his home during Vichy rule, like Karl Barth defined nazism as a "new Islam," but he was almost alone among the hierarchy.[10]

Both Protestants and Roman Catholics, in occupied countries as well as in Germany, were crippled in their confrontation with nazism by a traditional and church-centered view of Christian doctrine. Great numbers were led to pit "Christendom" over against "Bolshevik communism"; almost all were blind to the immediate values of secularized institutions and a pluralism of religious communities; even those who resisted were too narrow in their vision of the battlefield. Most of the hierarchy were like the pope himself, who "had no more ardent wish for the Führer than to see him gain a victory over Bolshevism."[11]

In the debate with heresy, most churchmen and theologians flunked their exams, and the minority who passed did so without distinction.

The Encounter with Political Antisemitism

Traditional Christianity (and most Christians) are locked in the level of theological and cultural Antisemitism, restrained by the teaching that—given enough suffering and wandering—the Jews would finally convert. In his important book *The Anguish of the Jews*, Father Edw. Flannery has reviewed the importance of this teaching in providing a tentative toleration for Jews in Christendom (before the collapse of Christian restraints, and the rise of "post-Christian" ideologies unabashedly Antisemitic and/ or anti-Zionist). He ascribes the origin of the teaching to Augustine: "Augustine's original contribution resides in his theory of the Jews as a witness people, a theological construction by which he attempts to solve the apparent dilemma of the Jews' survival as a people and their increasing misfortunes. . . . They are at once witnesses of evil and of Christian truth."[12] This provides, to be sure, a doctrinal hedge against outright murder of the Jews and was thus a restraint upon the hateful spirits released by a Cyprian or a Chrysostom. But in the West the doctrine was incapable of withstanding the force of modern political Antisemitism. It must be remembered too that Augustine's thought was never very important to Eastern Orthodoxy, where some of the most actively vicious Antisemitism has flourished.

The systematic assault upon the Jewish people began immediately upon Hitler's accession to power. The Enabling Act which made him dictator was passed March 24, 1933, and the first Antisemitic order was issued April 1. No Christian had a right to be surprised at the violent eruption of active, political Antisemitism in the heart of Christendom, in the centuries-old center of the Christian Roman Empire. A younger German scholar puts it succinctly: "The wiping out of the Jews would be inconceivable without the cooperation and participation of the Christians. It came neither suddenly nor unexpectedly. . . . It is no accident that the ideologues of Antisemitism have borrowed their weapons extensively from the arsenal of churchly teaching and terminology."[13] Those who made of Antisemitism a political weapon could mount it upon great barriers of theological and cultural Antisemitism built up by the churches.

Even more specifically, Antisemitism in its structured, legal form is part and parcel of Christendom, of the state-church system established by Constantine the Great. The French historian, Jules Isaac, concluded in one of his studies: "I say and maintain that the fate of Israel did not take on a truly inhuman character until the 4th century A.D. with the coming of the Christian Empire."[14] This is an additional reason why Christians who value religious liberty should be especially sensitive to oppression of the Jewish community.

Nor did the state-church Reformation lighten the burden of the Jews. Christianity has in recent years experienced no greater shame than that symbolized by the fact that the Nazis could reissue Martin Luther's attacks on the Jews without gloss or amendment. Three years before his death, Luther spewed forth Antisemitic bitterness and contempt in these words:

First, their synagogue or school is to be set on fire and what won't burn is to be heaped over with dirt and dumped on, so that no one can see a stone or chunk of it forever. . . . Second, their houses are to be torn down and destroyed in the same way. . . . Third, they are to have all their prayerbooks and Talmudics taken from them. . . . Fourth, their rabbis are to be forbidden henceforth to teach, on penalty of life and limb. . . . On penalty of life and limb, they are to be forbidden publicly to praise God, to thank (God), to pray (to God), to teach (of God) among us and ours. . . . And furthermore, they shall be forbidden to utter the name of God in our hearing; no value shall be accorded the Jewish mouth *(Maul)* by us Christians, so that he may utter the name of God in our hearing, but whoever hears it from a Jew shall report him to the authorities or throw pig droppings on him. . . . Fifth, the Jews are to be deprived totally of walkway and streets. . . . Sixth, they are to be forbidden lending for interest and all the cash and holdings of silver and gold are to be taken from them and put to one side for safe keeping. . . . Seventh, the young, strong Jews and Jewesses are to have flail, axe and spade put into their hands.[15]

It is still common, in many Protestant theological circles, either to pass over Luther's vituperative in silence or to attempt to pass it off as a "theological" statement which it is wrong to use politically. It was distinctly refreshing, therefore, to hear the president of the International Congress for Luther Research—a distinguished American scholar—say in his address at the Fourth Congress (St. Louis, August, 1971):

I have read—and indeed I have sometimes repeated—most of the conventional defenses of Luther's harsh language about the Jews: his disappointment that they did not accept the gospel now that it had been brought to light, his recognition of the difference between the believers of the Old Testament and the Jews after Christ, his indignation at the distortions of the Bible by rabbinical interpreters, and the like. Without minimizing the seriousness of any of these considerations, I cannot escape the conviction that the time has come for those who study Luther and admire him to acknowledge, more unequivocally and less pugnaciously than they have, that on this issue Luther's thought and language are simply beyond defense. But any such acknowledgement must be based, theologically, on a much more fundamental conviction, namely, that Judaism is not, as Luther and the centuries before him maintained, a "shadow" destined

to disappear with the coming of Christianity even though it stubbornly held on to its existence, but a permanent part of the won-
drous dispensation of God in human history.[16]

This is the beginning of a turnabout in the right direction. We
Protestants cannot ignore the fact that Julius Streicher could
quote Luther in his own defense at Nuremberg. Magisterial
Protestantism was just as hard on the Jews as the Latin church
had been, and in the twentieth century most Protestants joined
with most Roman Catholics to assist the murderers' game.

The Jews of Germany had, perhaps, more right to be surprised at the eruption of violent Antisemitism. Many of them
had, after the Emancipation, assimilated; the conversion rate to
the established Christian churches ran high. "It was above all
. . . hostility on the part of the outside world, and in particular
Christian opposition to emancipation, and later on the antisemitic movement, that prevented the total disintegration of
the Jews as a group."[17] The most enlightened political leaders,
in a time of enlightenment and progress, welcomed them into
intellectual concourse with other subjects of the Prussian king,
after 1871 Emperor of the Germans. The German Jews supposed that they were living in an age of progress, secure in a
society at the apex of modern civilization, a civilization which
would eventually accord them full rights and dignities. "Thus
the brutal and sudden awakening out of the illusion, out of the
dream of a solution to the Jewish question through liberalism
and eternal progress, was a terrible shock for German Jewry."[18]
The failure of assimilation in the most Christianized nation in
the world called the whole approach into question and gave
additional strength to the Zionist appeal. Those survivors who
had been unmoved by the call for a return to the Holy Land
were now forced to see that there were no practical alterna-
tives. The nations which professed horror at Hitler's brutality
toward the Jews were not ready to undertake emergency measures to save his victims. Political Antisemitism proved that
Herzl's dream of a Jewish state was a practical necessity, no
longer a romantic vision.

Resistance to mistreatment of "non-Aryan Christians" was at
first fairly extensive in both Protestant and Roman Catholic

church offices. After all, according to the New Testament, in Christ "is neither Jew nor Greek" (Galatians 3:28). Accommodation to Nazi policy was advocated very early by some officers, who proposed that separate congregations of Hebrew Christians be constituted. (The shipment of Jews to the Death Camps and the successful escape of a few from Germany made this solution unworkable.) A few churchmen resisted stoutly any breaking of Christian fellowship. In time, however, most church offices submitted; "non-Aryan" pastors and other officials were removed from office duty *(Amt)*, and the "non-Aryan" exclusion policies were accepted in the churches.[19] The remaining "Aryan" church officials were saved some immediate embarrassment by the steady disappearance of Jews from their communities.

Protests to general Antisemitic policy, to abuse and destruction of Jewry as such, were few and far between. Even the Confessing church was silent at Barmen (1934) and afterwards at Stuttgart (1945). The enervating principle was the pernicious doctrine that the duly constituted authorities were to be obeyed regardless of inner conscientious scruples. After the war, Lutherans like Bishop Berggrav of Norway and Bishop Dibelius of Berlin questioned whether the term *higher powers* (Romans 13:1) could properly be applied to those who had broken their oaths to the people under God. But even then their views were attacked by partisans of docility, and at the time of testing the views of the Lutheran professors at Erlangen were far more authoritative. The latter covered the scale from blatant Antisemitism to pragmatic arguments that the church should adopt the "non-Aryan" exclusion decrees for practical political reasons.

To obey God rather than men is a decision to which only a few Christians have been able to bring themselves.[20] In good part this is due to the fact that the church has had an inadequate body of writing and teaching on the duty of resistance to criminal governments and criminal actions by legitimate governments.[21] The commandant of Auschwitz stated: "I personally arranged on orders received from Himmler in May 1941 the gassing of two million persons between June–July 1941 and the end of 1943." In his autobiography Hoess wrote of his pious

Christian upbringing, of how he was taken to Lourdes and other shrines outside Germany, of how he was intended for the priesthood. Repeatedly he referred to his duty to obey orders, to carry out commands without question. The appearance of the serpent in the garden came early: "I can still remember how my father, who on account of his fervent Catholicism was a determined opponent of the Reich government and its policy, never ceased to remind his friends that, however strong one's opposition might be, the laws and decrees of the state had to be obeyed unconditionally."[22] Nothing Hoess was taught in a Christian home or in the church, to which he had as a boy more than usual connection, instructed him as to the time and place to say no to wicked commands.

This is still a great problem in the churches. There are now organized fellowships of pacifist Christians which reach far beyond the historic peace churches and take a general exception to war and violence. But for the nonabsolutist there is still a dearth of useful instruction and a minimum of support in crises of conscience.

Nor is this problem confined to the European established churches or uniquely to Germany. The writer will never forget the exchange with an American major general during the military occupation of postwar Germany. The American commander was declaiming loudly over the moral cowardice of the Germans in failing to resist Hitler. He was asked, "Then you mean, General, they should have been conscientious objectors to government policy?" Answer: "Certainly not: you can't have people refusing to obey orders." That this mentality still continues in strength—and the general was an upright man and a churchman—is shown by the Calley case and the vindictive policy of the U.S. government toward those who fled to avoid service in Vietnam.

Mennonites and Quakers and Brethren are fairly predictable in such crises of conscience. But would Christianity in America produce, under similar circumstances, more Bonhoeffers, Jägerstätters, von Motlkes, and Gersteins than did Christianity in Germany?

In America we have two great advantages as we begin to deal with illegal acts of government, of which genocide is the extreme example in this century. First, we have a constitutional recognition of the basic right of individuals and groups to religious liberty. The courts have in fact over the decades expanded the area of First Amendment liberties, of which what early Quakers called "soul liberty" is the most important. This means, not only that conscientious objection to participation in crimes against humanity is in principle secured at law, but that governmental power is deliberately restrained from making those claims to ultimate authority which were (and are) customary in both old-style sacral despotisms and new-style "post-Christian" dictatorships.

Second, we have in America a developing tradition of inter-religious cooperation, of which the National Conference of Christians and Jews (f. 1928) is the most significant and effective center. In recent years the NCCJ has moved beyond purely humanitarian and civic cooperation between Christians and Jews to work on the basic theological and historical reasons for alienation and grounds for mutuality.

In postwar Germany, *Gesellschaften für christlich-jüdische Zusammenarbeit* (societies for Christian-Jewish cooperation) were founded under the auspices of the Office of Religious Affairs and in cooperation with NCCJ staff from the United States. Although the work has continued, and in recent years the *Deutscher Evangelischer Kirchentag* has given major attention to rethinking Christian-Jewish relations, the problem is that there are very few Jews left in Germany. In fact, the critical question for Christianity in Germany is precisely whether it can advance in any meaningful way with virtually no Jewish presence left.

Recent studies show a rise in Antisemitism in the United States. Antisemitism has been called "the canary in the coalmine," a way to detect impending danger to the society as a whole. A rise of Antisemitism is often the first seismographic reading on a serious shifting and shearing along the fault lines of bedrock Christianity. The fundamental fault line, where yielding to pressure is most evident, is a line of false teaching about the Jewish people. Antisemitism serves a useful purpose to individuals insecure in their personal identity and to groups uncertain of their present and future prospects. It is therefore indicative of a broader and deeper malaise in the society and in the body politic.

The existence of Antisemitism also indexes the failure of Christian corporate life to provide a hope in which persons and groups can live constructively. The rise of modern political Antisemitism in the last century is thus a measure of the churches' failure to minister as well as to teach truthfully about the Jews. Not only the blood of the Jews but the blood of ill-trained and ill-served apostates must therefore be charged to the current account of Christendom. Antisemitism, like more general apostasy, is meshed with culture-religion, with religion which takes abstract positions but makes no specific claims.

Antisemitism provides an identity for individuals who would otherwise lack self-awareness. The Antisemite is in flight from the concrete and historical, the earthiness of human life and the finitude of human experience. Jean-Paul Sartre is certainly right in describing the collective revulsion against the limited size of the human measure, as in the Nazi passion for heroic buildings and "supermen." On the Antisemite, Sarte wrote:

> Incapable of understanding modern social organization, he has a nostalgia for periods of crisis in which the primitive community will suddenly re-appear and attain its temperature of fusion. He wants his personality to melt suddenly into the group and be carried away by the collective torrent.[23]

The reversion to the ethnic, to the tribal *Volksgemeinschaft*, in which personal decision and personal responsibility are swallowed up in a boundless popular passion, is the controlling spirit of totalitarian democracy. And totalitarian democracy, whether Fascist or Communist, is inexorably Antisemitic; even if Antisemitism (or "anti-Zionism") were not a substantial part of its conceptual baggage, the very rage against history would create it.

The Antisemite is a criminal in his heart and a coward in his public conduct.

> He is a man who is afraid. Not of the Jews, to be sure, but of himself, of his own consciousness, of his liberty, of his instincts, of his responsibilities, of solitariness, of change, of society, and of the world—of everything except the Jews.[24]

Toward the helpless, which in Christendom has usually meant the Jews, he directs a veritable torrent of contempt, hatred, and —when permitted—violence. In the passion of this moment, defined by the other, his disintegrating self converges like iron filings about a magnet. The Jew gives the Antisemite his identity as a kind of antimatter; his anxiety and self-hate is polarized in tension toward the one marked as a carrier of history.

The Jew, even if confused as an individual, has a historical identity. "Even if he denies his faith, a Jew nevertheless has a rendezvous with his Jewish destiny. Even if you flee from that destiny, it pursues you."[25] The Antisemite acquires a fleeting identity parasitically. These generalizations hold for Christians as well as other gentiles; the dangerous ones are the marginal Christians, those poised to break away from the church's gravitational field as soon as a more powerful pull sweeps by. Such a one is ready to move from cultural Antisemitism to active political Antisemitism. With very few exceptions, the active Christian Antisemites of the Third Reich were marginal men— socially as well as religiously—and they were often members of heretical movements. So too in the USA today: the active Antisemitic Christians are frequently sect leaders, disfrocked preachers, "clergymen" of uncertain ordination, vocal enemies of the major churches and of interchurch cooperation.

Thus while the Christian "establishments" can be fairly charged with theological and cultural Antisemitism, they are not directly guilty of political Antisemitism; this is carried by those who break away. The direction of the argument is fatally important. As the churches become aware that Antisemitism of any kind is a major sin, and this awareness is slowly growing in their midst, active Antisemitism becomes more and more the province of marginal men and movements. Just as Jewish self-hate drives most Jewish renegades, so active Antisemitism is a prime sign of Christian apostates. Although the church for long has taught lies about the Jewish people, and although many church leaders were too poisoned by those lies to stand up against the Russian pogroms and Nazi Holocaust of this century, the critical problem is lack of Christian discipline. With the erosion of Christian restraints, imperfect as they were, the plight of Jewry in Christendom became ever more precarious.

Those who carry Christian Antisemitism beyond the theological and cultural levels to the actively political offensive are products of Christianity, and a part of her sin and guilt, but they are breakaways from her ethos. As the revulsion against Antisemitism in all its forms grows in the heart of the churches, active Antisemites will be recognized for what they are: heretics and apostates, illegitimate rather than authentic expressions of Christian preaching and teaching.

Before this new level of Christian awareness can be reached, however, a long process of repentance, spiritual wrestling, and reform of preaching, teaching, and liturgy is required. Some practical suggestions were ventured in chapter 5, but the final answers must be given by the Holy Spirit working upon the life of the churches. The first step along the path of recovery is an honest facing of the earnestness of the fault and the peril of further neglecting correction. To date, the United Presbyterian church has an adequate report to its General Assembly which rethinks the Christian relation to the Jewish people. The National Council of Churches has recently appointed a competent man to direct an office on Christian-Jewish relations. American Catholics already have a Bishops' Commission on Christian-Jewish Affairs and an Institute of Judaeo-Christian Studies (Seton Hall University), both under superb and experienced direction. But what are other denominations doing? What are the seminaries and theological faculties doing? What are the church presses providing in lesson materials? So far, the answers are embarrassing.

In the debate with political Antisemitism and on the duty of Christian resistance to crimes against humanity, the churches failed in the time of testing (during Hitler's rise to power and his implementation of the Holocaust), and they are still well below the "passing" level today. This failure cannot be attributed to the German churches alone, nor to the churches of Vichy France and occupied Poland, nor even to the Roman Catholic, Lutheran, and Orthodox churches of the Ukraine and the Baltic states—from which came the most brutal of the Death Camp guards and executioners. English Christendom, which with a much smaller population and GNP had in 1685 taken in one hundred twenty thousand French Huguenots after

the revocation of the Edict of Nantes, by March, 1939, absorbed
only nineteen thousand Jews. American Christendom, although
the Federal Council of Churches once pleaded the cause of
Christian refugees from Germany, was passively set against
emergency measures to save Jewish lives. Sixty-six nations
refused help to Jewish refugees at the 1941 Bermuda Conference. Who shall stand among the innocent before a just and
righteous God?

The Agony of Doubt

After the war there was reported found among graffiti on the
wall of a cellar in Cologne where Jews had been hiding:

> I believe in the sun even when it is not shining.
> I believe in love even when feeling it not.
> I believe in God even when He is silent.

Such an affirmation is very hard for ordinary mortals to make.
Most cannot bear the eclipse of God, the silence of God—even
when it is deserved. We can sympathize readily with the cry of
a young girl herded toward the Nazi crematorium:

> Cold, God is cold; my hands grow numb
> When I try to fold them to pray with.[26]

According to Christian teaching, even Jesus himself was
wracked with the sense of forsakenness on the cross; had he not
been, no one could have called him completely human.

Six million Jews, sacrificed by the gentile world, lived and
died in a massive experience of abandonment from 1941 to
1945. This was an historical event. The Arab League spokesman
who denied the whole set of facts in the forum of the United
Nations, passing off the Holocaust as Jewish propaganda, was of
course displaying a certain resistance to evidence. More significant, he was taking the same stance toward the crucifixion of
European Jewry that he had been taught to take toward the
crucifixion of Jesus of Nazareth. On Jesus' death, Muhammad
said, "but they did not kill him, and they did not crucify him,
but a similitude was made for them. . . . They did not kill him,
for sure!"[27] A religion to which immediate worldly success is a

direct corollary to religious orthodoxy, a religion which flees from the awful and the mysterious, a religion in which the Suffering Servant plays no part—neither as a model for individuals nor as a force in history—cannot bear to hear about crucifixion.

That is to say, American culture-Christianity—with its "positive thinking," its "cheap grace" and "easy conversions"—is blind to the meaning of the crucifixion of the Jews, just as it has gaily turned what happened at Golgotha into a vulgar success story, assuring us that Jesus was a "winner" after all! Culture-religion is a form of Islam, only awaiting an inspired prophet to turn it into the wildly Antisemitic and demonic crusade of which nazism under its *Führer* was a prime example.

We Christians have been taught to affirm the formative meaning of certain events of the past. We have been taught to read Isaiah 53, for example, as predictive of an event consummated and closed off at the Place of the Skulls. If we should come to understand, however, that the mysterious actions of God continue in this history, and that history is not a desolate wasteland without event or meaning between Pentecost and the Last Judgment, how then should we behold the appearance of the Suffering Servant? Read Isaiah 53 along with "O, the Chimneys" by Nelly Sachs, or Kaplan's *Scroll of Agony*, or . . . *I never saw another butterfly!*

To attempt to ascribe simple meanings to an event like the crucifixion of Jesus or the crucifixion of European Jewry is very dangerous. The devout response is instinctive: "Woe is me! for I am undone; because I am a man of unclean lips, and I dwell in the midst of a people of unclean lips: for mine eyes have seen the King, the Lord of hosts" (Isaiah 6:5). Yet we have been freed to debate with God, and in faith we may perceive the dim outlines of a transcendent meaning emerging from the Holocaust. A Jewish scholar has pointed out one profound truth about the redemptive work of the sacrificed Jews:

> Had the Nazis not been racist, they still would have been evil—and infinitely more dangerous, for then they would have found their natural fascist allies among all races of men. So in order to bring them low—"Whom God would destroy he first makes mad"—the

genocidal but self-defeating madness of racism was an indispensible ingredient of Nazism. The Jews, God's perpetually willing instrument, paid the terrible price, serving as the racist target in order to save mankind from the Nazi scourge; the reward to the remnants, three years later, was the return to Zion.[28]

In time to come there will be other meanings as well to be drawn from the work of the Suffering Servant. In the meantime the debate with God, the battle with the spiritual blindness which overshadows the age, calls us to return again and again in prayer and reflection to reports of the Event.

The agony of doubt, of possible abandonment by God, is enhanced by the knowledge of abandonment by other men. This too was part of Christendom's crime against the Jews shipped to the Death Camps. The feeling of desertion is frequently expressed in journals and letters that have survived. One person who outlived Auschwitz has written of that shock, "I did not believe they could burn people in our age, [I believed] that humanity would never tolerate it."[29] But "humanity" did not exist, and the nations not only tolerated it, they were actively or passively implicated in the deed, as is discussed in books such as Henry L. Feingold's *The Politics of Rescue: The Roosevelt Administration and the Holocaust, 1938–1945*, Arthur D. Morse's *While Six Million Died: A Chronicle of American Apathy*, and Gordon Zahn's *German Catholics and Hitler's Wars*. The facts were kept from the public by Churchill and FDR and Pius XII, as well as by Hitler and Mussolini. The Vichy French collaborated in gathering the Jews for the Nazi "final solution." Poles and Russians shot Jews who escaped to join the anti-Nazi partisans and, in fact, continued their purges and pogroms after Hitler was dead and the Third Reich went down in flames. "When the Nazis killed a third of our people, just men found nothing to say."[30]

The wickedness of politicians, churchmen, and editors, as painful as it is, is only traumatic to those who rely on a falsely optimistic view of human nature and social progress. To those who have measured the wickedness of men, including church leaders, the pussyfooting of politicians and the moral cowardice of ecclesiastics is initially a shock, but it carries no final trauma. In the rich religious resources of the *stetl*, a Jewish island surrounded by a gentile sea, East European Jewry found enough strength to endure destruction, and its few select survivors come among us today as teachers and professors of biblical truths we of Christendom had almost forgotten.

Neither does the irruption of false gods and the prosperity of false prophets produce doubt in the depths of one's being. It is painful for a Protestant to see high churchmen who are unworthy of their posts, even more painful for Catholics to have to remember a pope who betrayed the office hallowed by the blood of martyrs and confessors. For a professor, it is a wretched experience to review the records of Hitler's professors, to tot up the Antisemitism of some of his own teachers, to consider the extent to which the same wicked lies about the Jews which made the Holocaust possible are still taught in seminaries and theological faculties. Elie Wiesel has written ironically of the world which denies memory and tradition, which repudiates any truth beyond human manipulation, which needs "new gods and new religions" because then only the survivors have "the right to decide what is good and what is evil."[31] Yet this is not the deepest layer of agony; gods come and go, idols rise and fall, religious prophets and priests bloom and wither.

The deepest agony arises from the thought that God himself is an ally of evil, that he is "capable of the most flagrant injustice,"[32] that he may appear on the compass of one's life standing directly behind the Adversary. The appalling thought arises that one must choose between a cruel God or none.[33] It is here that the "Death of God" theologians made their choice, a choice which—even if proven unnecessary—was at least more morally earnest than the frivolous replies they generally received. "My God is alive: sorry about yours," the sticker which appeared on bumpers of some automobiles was intellectually and spiritually at the same level as much of the response by American churchmen.[34]

The crisis of faith precipitated by the Holocaust runs more broadly than the credibility crisis in Christianity. "The mountain of misery created by the Nazi holocaust poses a major problem for the traditional Biblical faith that God works in history, and for its corollary that His righteousness is manifest in human affairs."[35]

We are back to Grüber and Rubenstein,[36] where, if we may venture to predict, the philosophical battle will be fought out for a long time. But the terrain is disadvantageous; the Adversary has won all the skirmishes; some of the most valiant champions have been carried away by death; our forces are poorly deployed and tormented by a pervading sense of widespread defection in the ranks. Most of all, the philosophical battle is only tangentially related to the struggle for religious benediction. The central issue is not to reaffirm with revitalized assensus an orthodox proposition; neither is it to give heroic affirmation to an abstraction that saves ethics at the cost of fellowship with one's fathers and fathers' fathers. The debate with God is best carried forward not in pursuit of direct encounters with an unmediated divinity, but through dealing—in all human vigor and with all human limitations—with the concrete issues and decisions affecting one's fellows and one's self. The insistent question is not whether God exists, nor whether his ways make sense in terms of known systems of thought. The insistent question is what must be done here and now by specific persons facing specific choices. Knowing who we are and where we are, we may from time to time see his glory passing by, or later mark where he has been (Exodus 33:21–23). We do ill, indeed act presumptuously, in spending time in pursuit of direct encounters with the Divine which the Bible instructs us to devote to service to his people and to the neighbor.

I cannot pretend to define for Jews the meaning of the Holocaust. The Antisemites and their hidden helpers have been moralizing to the Jews to the point where Christian credibility is at best highly attenuated. But concerning the nature of the crisis in Christianity, in which I daily participate, I will exercise my liberty to speak. The Jewish people, who have in our time experienced crucifixion and resurrection, have their own prophets and teachers. The Christians, who fled the time of testing, who have refused as yet to face the truth of their apostasy, who are still trying to fly high with abstract resolutions and generalizations, must be brought to book. The Jews, having passed through the fire, are seeing the prophecy of Isaiah fulfilled:

> And he shall set up an ensign for the nations,
> and shall assemble the outcasts of Israel,
> and gather together the dispersed of Judah
> from the four corners of the earth.
>   (Isaiah 11:12)

The Christians, having drunk deeply of the cup of staggering, slide from one fad to another—peace, social justice, civil rights for homosexuals, women's lib—anything but admission of guilt and rebellion against God, and the turning again which could make their attention to such matters a Christian witness rather than a program gimmick.

The Continuing Church Struggle

Following World War I, the German Protestants thought they knew who their enemies were: communism, liberalism, and Roman Catholicism.[37] Like the radical right in America, the Nazi ideologues aimed their most severe blows against the "liberals." "Liberalism is the expression of a society that is no longer a community. . . . Every man who no longer feels a part of the community is somehow a liberal man."[38] The German rightists were primitivists:[39] the Lost Eden to be recaptured was the ethnic community of Teutonic tribalism. They were therefore the enemies of structured, mature social institutions, of bureaucracies and due process of law. Since many of the German Protestants, with a spirit like those who dream of a lost "Christian America" today, were constantly recalling the glories of the Christian monarchy before the Weimar Republic, they were psychologically prepared to follow the reactionary, primitivist call of a Hitler. What he proclaimed publicly—against liberalism, against "Bolshevism," against parliamentarianism, against internationalism and cosmopolitanism; for the restoration of Germanic glory and *Volksgemeinschaft,* for "nonsectarian religion"—sounded to the baptized masses very much like what their preachers had said all along.

The irony of the German Catholic role is that, like so many American Catholics who have followed the radical right, they did not realize that in the old-fashioned "Christian Germany" or "Christian America" there is no place for Catholics either.

When Prelate Kaas, head of the Center party, cast the decisive vote to make Hitler a dictator (March 24, 1933), he thought he was striking a blow against "secularism," liberalism, and communism and securing Catholic interests by the impending Concordat; in fact, he was both betraying the Republic and sacrificing the interests of his church. By 1937 this was so evident that Pius XI issued *Mit brennender Sorge* to protest Nazi failure to live up to formal agreements.

If the churchmen of Germany thought they knew who their enemies were—the "secular" winning out over the "spiritual," structured institutions growing in strength, while old tribal and patriarchal patterns lost authority—they were profoundly uncertain as to what they believed and where the source of their professed truth was to be found. The scientific analysis of religious traditions and texts was more advanced in German theology than in any other country. In the authoritative references, such as the great encyclopedia, *Die Religion in Geschichte und Gegenwart*, the Old Testament was presented as Jewish folklore and fable and the authority of both Old and New Testament thoroughly relativized. Abstractions about "religion" had replaced storytelling among the educated. Among the masses, on the other hand, although the oral tradition was quite eroded, there remained the area of "inner experience," of "sincere conviction"—which German teachers since Schleiermacher had reserved as the center of intellectually respectable religion. The overall picture in Protestantism was one of an elite believing in very little except the scientific method and masses believing much of religion-in-general but little of concrete historical events. The professors were in poor shape to resist a dynamic new ideology at least of equal status to other creeds and religions; the baptized masses were unable to tell the difference between one "inner experience" and another, between the emotion aroused by a Pietist meeting and the atmosphere of a party rally.

The dynamic thrust of the Nazi movement resolved the agony of doubt for both intellectuals overcome by the vertigo of their own "higher criticism" ("the higher Antisemitism," Rabbis Hirsch and Schechter had called it), and the baptized masses, who understood that real religion has sentiment, pas-

sion, sincerity, mystery, power, enthusiasm, sacrifice, commitment—but respected little if any intellectual discipline.[40] Ra-
tionalism and Pietism, thus balanced and structured in German
Protestantism, were ill-prepared to represent Christianity on a
spiritual battlefield like the Church Struggle. The confessional
orthodoxy which yet existed in some centers was dehydrated,
largely uninteresting to the intellectuals and uninspiring to the
masses. An important reason why so much of the energy of the
Confessing church went into dogmatic issues is precisely that
confrontation with nazism required a rethinking and reworking
of creedal and confessional declarations generally beyond the
spiritual energy and intellectual capacity of those who had
maintained a fossilized form of Christian truth. Confessions of
faith, if they are truly orthodox, are not "dead" at all; they are
battlefield orders, not seldom abrupt and fragmented rather
than well-rounded and comprehensive.

That liberal Protestantism is also ill-suited to confront the
radical right here and to deal with the religion-in-general which
it sponsors, that for more than a decade the major church agencies have refused to look at the fact that we are now living in
the preliminary stages of a church struggle which has steadily
grown in intensity since 1958 and which has already cost
heavily in reduced budgets and dismissed personnel, is due to
our failure to master the lessons of the Church Struggle and the
Holocaust. A very well-written and intelligent book by an
American churchman may be quoted to make the point, to
illustrate how fully American culture-Christianity is still lodged
in the nineteenth century. He is vigorously opposed to confessions of faith and devoted to "the basic faith-mood of man which
flows in his conscience like a great underground stream of water." Reporting a religious experience in contemplation of one
of the beauties of Nature, the Dawn, he writes: "Beholding such
loveliness, feeling more than understanding its meaning, like
the inquirer who stands before unfolding truth, you would
speak, but no words come, for no words can serve your purpose.
Then a Name rises to your lips, an ancient name, a name as old
as man. And so you speak the Name, not knowing quite what
you have said or why you have said it."[41] There is indeed something very religious about this Unknown God and in the ecstatic

utterance with which he is greeted. Paul met him among the crowds on Mars Hill and was not unwilling to walk that verbal bridge to help their understanding (Acts 17:22 f.). But in times of church struggle, when the foundations are shaken and the axe is laid at the root of every tree, this is a weak support to stand upon.

Eugen Rosenstock-Huessy, the friend and dialogist with Franz Rosenzweig, has told of the incident in his life which made him decide to emigrate from Germany. In 1933 he was visited in Berlin by a friend, a pastor from Westphalia, who told him that all Rosenstock had wanted was accomplished: work camps, work communities, reform of the academic spirit, and so forth. Only one thing must be understood: "Hitler is the Christ." This blasphemy, so symbolic of nazism, decided his leaving.[42]

But if in "religion" you speak a name "not knowing quite what you have said," why shouldn't the name be "Adolf Hitler"? For many, this was a way to resolve the agony of doubt without coming to terms with the genuine contributions of the scientific study of religion(s), without balancing inner emotion with intellectual discipline (in new confessions of faith).

The Church Struggle, confronting us with the crisis of political Antisemitism and the undertow of a formless "spirituality," demands not only increased devotion to the faith but courageous intellectual wrestling with the findings of modern science. The true confession of faith "cannot be authoritative for the Church's doctrine and life *ad omnem posteritatem* but only 'until further notice.' The Confession is debatable, improvable, and replaceable. Reformed dogma is in a fluid state; it is dogma only in an act of knowledge that is to be renewed over again."[43] This means that old and outdated creeds, "dead" orthodoxies, are inadequate in the moment of confrontation and decision, and also that new confessions must not claim for themselves more authority than human persons in their finitude can honorably affirm. But it also means that Christianity-in-earnest cannot burke the responsibility to think Christianly and to act decisively along lines defined by both mind and emotion. It means that those who have died in the faith are in the debate with us as well as are those present and accounted for.

Robert Welch has clearly stated his version of *positives Christentum:*

> I am not in favor of trying to reimpose all or any of the strands of
> a fundamentalist faith on those whose reason, right or wrong, has
> honestly told them that we cannot know such positive things about
> the Unknowable. For that would be like trying to tie the waves of
> the ocean together with ropes, or to confine them with fishing nets.
> But I believe there is a broader and more encompassing faith to
> which we can all subscribe, without any of us doing the slightest
> violation to the more specific doctrines of his own creed or altars of
> his own devotion. And I believe it is an ennobling conception,
> equally acceptable to the most fundamentalist Christian or the most
> rationalistic idealist, because its whole purport is to strengthen and
> synthesize the ennobling characteristics of each man and the enno-
> bling impulses of his own personal religion. . . .
> It is hard for man to realize that the Infinite still remains infinite,
> untouched in Its remoteness and unreduced in Its infinity by man's
> most ambitious approaches; or that all of man's increasing knowl-
> edge leaves the Unknowable just as completely unknowable as
> before.
> Look with me first at the common denominators of all of our great
> religions . . . and a reverence for a Power or Powers greater than
> man himself. . . . But, gentlemen, please note, these are also exactly
> the characteristics with which evolutionary selection has gradually
> endowed man, to enable him to rise out of an animal existence.[44]

If the vaguely "spiritual" and "religious" language isn't enough
to identify Welch's type of thought, the final note of social
Darwinism should be. This is heresy, where found within the
churches.

In view of this, and especially in light of the heavy losses
suffered by church agencies in the developing struggle, it is
astonishing that the denominations have by and large ignored
the nature of the attacks. They have given them no consistent
theological—and very little practical—attention. This means
that they have not studied the recent Church Struggle in Germany and other parts of Nazi-occupied Europe. It means too
that they are still weighted down by the style of abstract thinking which makes flight from concrete historical crises, confrontations, and difficult decisions almost automatic.

The truth is that Antisemitism (at the active, political level), low-grade "confessionless Christianity," and other widespread indiscipline and disaffection among both laity and clergy is evidence of years of poor preaching, inadequate teaching, and relaxed internal discipline. In place of real reform, the church agencies turn instead to schemes for livelier and more appealing programs, better methods of promotion, more energetic drives and campaigns. Behind all this is the false assumption that nothing is fundamentally wrong, that the problem is to do better and more enthusiastically what we are already doing.

This false assumption, in an age in which the churchmen have dodged the debate with heresy, flubbed the encounter with Antisemitism, relaxed church discipline all along the line, recognized the face of the Adversary too seldom and too late, and supported wicked acts of governments almost without exception, derives from the flight from history—past, present, and future.

The basic nature of the church as a pilgrim people, as a community of disciplined witness, as a general priesthood living in anticipation of a better age to come, is lost from vision. Since the Christians misunderstand so much about their own history, they frequently find the first people of the Scriptures an enigma. Since many Jews are not "spiritual" in the way Christians define "spirituality," many Christians conclude the Jews are "secularistic" and not "truly religious." But the Bible does not speak of the "spiritual," the "material," the "secular," the "religious" in this way. The doctrines of the incarnation and the resurrection should be enough, standing by themselves, to hedge Christian thought against such error. That they do not is proof positive of how little the basic Christian beliefs, let alone the virtually unopened Bible,[45] have to do with the current mindset of culture-Christianity in America.

After the liberation of Old Jerusalem from nineteen years of illegal Jordanian occupation, an Israeli airman who had been educated to atheism remarked: "I had the feeling that I would like to bring all my ancestors, through all the generations, and say to them, 'Look, I'm standing by the Western Wall.' "[46] Ostensibly atheist or no, this young Israeli was far closer to biblical faith than much of the emancipated, confessionless, and formless "Christianity" which dominates American culture-religion. To have faith is to remember, to recapitulate, to reenact primordial events; it means among other things to accept the life which is given, in its concrete and historical specificity. Christians of the Enlightenment, who have pursued so relentlessly the timeless truths and placeless abstractions that ring in the ear but never move the feet, could learn much about true faith from this young "atheist."

Christendom, with its docetic "spirituality" and nonhistorical abstractions, has invented such antiseptic rules of self-deception as "final solution" and political lies "no longer operative." Elie Wiesel has described a scene in which the abstract, the mechanical, the deadly triumphed: "[The official] missed no opportunity to remind those refugee fellows that their status was subhuman. In that enormous hall, the ancient question was finally answered: 'What is a human being? Someone whose papers are in order.' "[47] Jewry, with its very material and historical consciousness, has preserved the human person with a real countenance. He is not primarily a primate with an opposable thumb. He is not primarily a toolmaker. He is not primarily a form with a "spirit" which will eventually return to the Unknown and Unknowable, like a drop of water to the ocean. He is a creature with a memory, with a self-awareness which transcends himself and, placing him in time and space, gives him his identity.

Both Jews and Christians have given a Name to that transcendence although the former are more careful than the latter that the Name is not bandied about cheaply. The thrust of Christian "spiritualizers" ends in the dehumanization of masses of men and turns the elite into "supermen" above the Law. The memories of Jewish "materialists," relived in the present, restore the human measure and make understanding and compassion and love possible between human persons. A lively memory of the Law of God, refreshed by a vital oral tradition, is widely present in Jewry today but sadly eroded in Christian circles. In Christendom of the twentieth century, fleeing from history and remembered events, the new and apocalyptic figures of prestige have come to be disloyal generals, lawless policemen, false prophets, professors who do not profess, and public servants who do not serve.

Alienation and Recovery

The natural alienation of the individual comes with passage through puberty to mature manhood or womanhood. It is important to note, although it does not affect the direction of our argument, that in industrial societies the age of individual transition has been pressed downward in the last century: that is menstruation began at seventeen and one-half years in 1880 and now begins at twelve and four-tenths years. At this point the person normally becomes aware of the disjointedness of life, of his disjarment from the previously intact world. He finds himself at odds with nature, in tension with the previous generations, in doubt about the meaning of his life. He is aware of what the psychologists call "alienation" and what the theologians call "sin."[48]

Until this crossing of the frontier a person was able to memorize easily; he could learn "instinctively" to ride a horse, drive a car, sing a song, handle a gun, speak a foreign language. With adulthood, especially among persons trained to a high level of scientific reflection and analysis, these enterprises become difficult to pick up. If he has not already accumulated a substantial fund of the oral tradition (whether Scriptures, poetry, song, drama, stories, or tales), he enters adulthood deprived. His dialogue with life's meaning will be more and more dependent upon the merely contemporary; "racial memory" will recede and eventually disappear.

Science is thus a product of what theologians have traditionally called "the fall." In innocence, the individual has no sense of lostness; he has no identity problem. Imitating his elders without debate, he is as much at home with mystery and the unexplained as he is imitating the making of a tool or preparation of a meal. In maturity, his doubting mind races to analyze, to invent, to correlate evidences apparently unrelated, to critique. If he gives attention over many years to nothing but "scientific method" (whether as doctor, teacher, or mechanic;

whether in the analysis of music, musicology; or the comparison of social forces and institutions, sociology; or the abstraction of laws of behavior in the material world, physics), he may become the typical product of our modern educational system: a technically competent barbarian. If he gives sole attention to memorizing and perpetuating received truths, he will not become a mature person fit for a changing world, and eventually the lessons memorized, having outlived their time and place, will dehydrate and be blown away by more powerful myths and tales. A sound education, adequate for mature persons, will feature both Science *(techne)* and Wisdom (not *sophia* alone, but also *logos).*

In the dialogue with the Book of Nature, the adult person will devise experiments and inventions to make the natural world yield up its secrets and its treasures. He will also, if wise, respect his materials and carefully steward the resources over which he has been given dominion.

In the dialogue with the Book of History, he will look to reliable sources, accumulate and marshal evidence in careful and judicious spirit. He will also carry on the dialogue with the past in careful attention to the decisions of the present and in the light of his hope for the future. For "history" is not a pile of dead facts at which he looks; history is something which he also does.

In the dialogue with the Book of Books, he will maintain the tension between the oral tradition and analysis, between storytelling and textual criticism, between the wealth of inherited wisdom which he memorized as a child and the critical insights which he has acquired as an adult.

And in all of these dialogues, if he would be healed and made whole, he will welcome interaction with others who are engaged in the same enterprises in the light of the spirit of truth. This is especially the case if the other person or persons have lived through the same set of experiences and may contribute precisely the needed catalyst to make a fuller sense of one's own memories.

The misery of the present Christian situation is that, having over centuries looked at the Jewish people from a soundproof

room installed with one-way windows, the church cannot yet
find the moral strength to step through the door and learn from
the Jews the present meanings of crucifixion and resurrection.
Within the stifling atmosphere of the closed room the same old
phrases still echo against the walls as they are flung about, but
with increasing frequency the words are jumbled and the individual psyche responds with an automatic cutout. Masses are
ripe for apostasy. Others are stepping outside the four walls and
engaging in dialogue with persons of other faiths. Especially
important, and to be welcomed by churchmen yet alive, is the
swelling number of groups engaged in Christian-Jewish dialogue. For at a number of critical points the Jewish people have
the specific medicine to cure our malaise.

Jewry was not saved out of the Holocaust by assimilation into
the gentile world, but by a tradition of fully human response to
God's will. At its spiritually most courageous, this tradition produced the debate with God. Whether, once the Christians begin to learn from the Jews, this dimension of great, living faith
can be built into Christian religious life remains to be seen.
Although Christianity has not gone so far as Islam ("the submission") in making utter and unquestioning acceptance of whatever happens a religious virtue, still Christians have not usually
been trained to wrestle with the angel, to question what happens under God's sovereignty. Christian mystics, like Muslim
faithful, have raised obedience, submission, and acceptance of
one's fate *(Gelassenheit, gelijdsamheid)* to religious virtues.
Among the Jews of the Hasidic tradition, however, the debate
with God was cultivated and carried right into the Death
Camps.[49]

If man is man, and ought neither to arrogate to himself divine
authority nor to wallow in self-contempt in the life he has been
given, if his maturity requires both the critical and the devo-
tional, the analytical and also courageous commitment to ultimate things, then the model of the debate with God affords a
working approach to his conduct in faith. The janitor in a Jewish
synagogue in the *stetl* who challenges God because he is absent
while his people appear before the altar deserves to be matched
by a Christian layman who will demand to know why he was led

into temptation—ill-trained, unformed, undisciplined!

The lay Christian, who according to the Bible shares in the general ministry by virtue of his baptism, cannot place the blame on the church leaders because in the time of testing he slid into Antisemitic violence, ethnic chauvinism, radical right disloyalty, apostasy, although in the end the faithless shepherds will answer to a Higher Judge. He knows, if he carries the debate with God through to its final moment, that he was personally responsible that he did not pray resolutely enough, did not stand to the cross courageously enough, did not love ardently enough. The debate with God thus becomes an intensely personal matter, which he must live personally just as he must go personally to his earthly death.

The Essential Jewishness of Christianity

The recovery of Christian integrity and credibility in the historical process does not depend upon more sturdy affirmations about our indebtedness to Jewish foundations. It depends upon what happens now and in time to come in interaction between the two peoples.

Dr. Robert L. Lindsey, a Southern Baptist scholar who has spent many years serving in Jerusalem, has proposed a solution to the mystery of Christian-Jewish interaction in the holy history to which both peoples belong and in which both play vital roles. As a Free Church man and an evangelist in the New Testament sense, he rejects the whole concept of "Christendom" and the territorial definition of "Christianity" and "Christians." He is troubled by the problem posed by large masses of nominal Christians, just as he is troubled by the failure of traditional Christian teaching about the Jewish people.

> Who are these nominal Christians? Where did they come from? Quite simply, they are our brethren "according to the flesh." They are the children and grandchildren of people who called themselves Christians. . . . Were the Apostle Paul living today he would doubtless say about these masses that God "loves them because of their fathers." He would not call them saved or chosen.
> . . . There really cannot be any kind of Christianity which is not

Jewish. . . . One can quite simply claim that all Christians are Jews (on the plane of Holy History) but not all Jews are Christians (on the plane of chosenness or salvation).[50]

Outside the circle of intimate historical purpose there are "gentiles"—persons belonging neither to the Jewish people nor to the Christian churches, having as yet no express purpose in God's action in history. Many of them are baptized.

This resolution of the immediate theological problems has a number of virtues: it overpowers and supplants the superseding myth; it outlaws Antisemitism among Christians; it distinguishes between nominal Christians—whose marginality of attachment is a major weakness of embattled Christianity—and the genuine article; it ties Jews and Christians together in an unbreakable bond. Yet, as appealing as the solution is in view of his earlier training, the present writer cannot use it in his debate with God. There flows a river of fire between: the Holocaust.

The Holocaust is the unfinished business of the Christian churches, the running sore unattended by its leaders and weakening to its constituents. The most important event in recent generations of church history, it is still virtually ignored in church school lessons and carefully avoided by preachers in their pulpits. More than anything else that has happened since the fourth century, it has called into question the integrity of the Christian people and confronted them with an acute identity crisis. They have not yet reestablished their right to a blessing and a name; so Dr. Lindsey's theological solution is too early for Jews to welcome and Christians to comprehend. The identity crisis will not be finally mastered, if at all, until the prayers and hymns and antiphonies of Christian congregational worship memorialize those who perished for the sake of the Holy Name at the hands of the rebellious, apostate gentiles of Christendom. Above all, before we Christians "define" the Jewish people again, we have a long way to go in atonement for our sins and guilt, many credible actions to produce before we verbalize freely again, and a great deal to learn about Biblical faith precisely from contemporary Jewry.

Once the human and genteel level is surpassed, the breakdown of basic communication between Jews and Christians still yawns wide. Christians have difficulty in understanding that the passage through the Holocaust to a restored Israel is for the Jewish people comparable to crucifixion and resurrection. And the difficulty is not just blindness toward recent Jewish history; it arises because proud church establishments have no place for either crucifixion or resurrection in their self-understanding. Jews have difficulty in accepting the thought that the cross might be a sign of ultimate victory because their treatment by the Christians has made it something quite different and immediate; for the Jews, the Christian cross is a sign of crusading slaughter, pogroms, and mass murder.

If the Christians in self-defense and self-justification reply that the cross is misunderstood by the Jews, that from where they stand looking on the cross glows with peace and joy, the Jews may justly reply that they have experienced themselves the blood and the shame and the passion and would rather live with a mystery than utter a hollow-sounding proposition. In Christendom, which was where the crime of the Holocaust was committed, very few Christians—with the notable exception of the black congregations—can today speak authentically of the cross. And the Jews, who have experienced the cross on a vast scale, with the loss of one-third of their total world population in three years (1942–45), see the cross as something that Christians do to others.

The Christians have no one to blame but themselves that Christianity is incredible to the Jews and to many gentiles who have fraternally shared in the recent history of the Jewish people. The Christians have no one to condemn but themselves that the cross remains a sign of boundless human cruelty rather than an arrow of hope pointing to the final victory of the Kingdom of God.

My Jewish friend has

no doubt that if masses of Christians in Hitler's Europe had voluntarily put on the yellow star there would today be no doubt or confusion in the Christian churches, no talk of the death of God. I also have an uncanny feeling that Christians might find the renewal they presently seek if . . . their souls were to enter into the despair and the hope-despite-despair of Auschwitz.[51]

And he is much more a brother of mine than those who triumphantly cover their nakedness by appealing to the good works of Bonhoeffer, Delp, von Moltke, Schneider, and all the others. We were not worthy of them then, and we are not worthy of them now. I would far rather stand with my Jewish friend in the end, before the Bar of Judgment, than to have to answer not only for my guilt as a Christian in 1941–45 but for latterly peddling cheap grace as well.

When the Body of Christ is discovered at Auschwitz, it will be raised from among the victims, not hidden among the Catholic and Protestant and Orthodox guards and administrators. When the Messiah comes to consummate the longings and hopes of all mankind, he will be of the lineage of Abraham and David, not a timeless and faceless wraith, his head wreathed in abstractions.

And I believe that though he tarry yet he will come!

NOTES

1. Faith statement of the *Deutsche Christen,* a document published in *Kirchliches Jahrbuch,* ed. Joachim Beckmann (Gütersloh: C. Bertelsmann Verlag, 1948), p. 491 f.

2. Wolfgang Gerlach, "Kreuz und Davidstern," (Ph.D. diss., University of Hamburg, 1972), p. 20.

3. Otto Kopp, ed., *Widerstand und Erneuerung* (Stuttgart: Seewald Verlag, 1966), p. 90.

4. Document in the National Archives: T–175, Roll 271, Frame 27767026.

5. W. A. Visser't Hooft, ed., *The Struggle of the Dutch Church* (New York: American Committee for the World Council of Churches, 1943), pp. 72–73.

6. Cf. Franklin H. Littell, "The Secular City and Christian Self-Restraint," in *The Church and the Body Politic* (New York: Seabury Press, 1969), ch. 6.

7. Gerlach, "Kreuz und Davidstern," pp. 492–96.

8. For one set of reports on Headlam's activity see William A. Visser't Hooft, *Die Welt war meine Gemeinde* (Munich: R. Piper & Co., 1972), p. 103 f.

9. Alexander Werth, *France, 1940–1955* (New York: Henry Holt & Co., 1956), p. 60.

10. Saul Friedländer, *Pius XII and the Third Reich: A Documentation* (London: Chatto & Windus, 1966), p. 55 f; also frontispiece letter.

11. Reported to Berlin by the German ambassador, von Weizsäcker; ibid., p. 85.

12. Edw. H. Flannery, *The Anguish of the Jews* (New York: Macmillan Co., 1964), p. 50.

13. Hans-Jürgen Schultz, ed., *Juden/ Christen/ Deutsche* (Stuttgart: Kreuz-Verlag, 1961), p. 2.

14. Jules Isaac, *Has Anti-Semitism Roots in Christianity?* (New York: National Conference of Christians and Jews, 1961), p. 45.

15. Martin Luther: *Von den Juden und ihren Lügen* (1543).

16. *CCI Notebook* No. 4 (October 1971), p. 2, from address by Prof. Jaroslav Pelikan.

17. Walter Laqueur, *A History of Zionism* (New York: Holt, Rinehart & Winston, 1970), p. 19.

18. Werner Feilchenfeld, Dolf Michaelis, and Ludwig Pinner, *Havara-Transfer nach Pälestina und Einwanderung Deutscher Juden 1933–1939* (Tübingen: J. C. B. Mohr, 1972), p. 16.

19. In 1933 there were only twenty-nine pastors of "non-Aryan" descent (.0019 percent); there had been only ninety-eight since the Reformation; 38 *Deutsches Pfarrerblatt* (1933) 44:765.

20. For the story of one of the most noble Christian witnesses, see Gordon C. Zahn, "He Would Not Serve," in *America* (5 July 1958), pp. 385–90, and Zahn's biography of Jägerstätter: *In Solitary Witness* (New York: Holt, Rinehart & Winston, 1964).

21. Cf. Bernhard Pfister and Gerhard Hildmann, eds., *Widerstandsrecht und Grenzen der Staatsgewalt* (Berlin: Duncker & Humblot, 1956).

22. Rudolf Hoess, *Commandant of Auschwitz: The Autobiography of . . .* (Cleveland: World Publishing Co., 1959), pp. 17, 32.

23. Jean-Paul Sartre, *Anti-Semite and Jew* (New York: Schocken Books, 1965), p. 3.

24. Ibid., p. 53.

25. Avraham Shapira et al., *The Seventh Day* (London: Penguin Books, 1971), p. 241.

26. Rolf Hochhuth, *The Deputy* (New York: Grove Press, 1964), p. 226.

27. E. Palmer, trans., *The Qur'an* (Oxford: Clarendon Press, 1880), p. 281.

28. "A Martyrology of the Holocaust," prepared for Yom Kippur 5370 (1969), by Dr. Robert Wolfe; personal correspondence with the author.

29. Elie Wiesel, *Night* (New York: Avon Books, 1969), p. 19.

30. Elie Wiesel, *Dawn* (New York: Avon Books, 1970), p. xv.

31. Elie Wiesel, *The Accident* (New York: Avon Books, 1970), p. 96.

32. Elie Wiesel, *A Beggar in Jerusalem* (New York: Avon Books, 1971), p. 45.

33. Robert Gordis, "A Cruel God or None—Is There No Other Choice?" 21 *Judaism* (1972) 3:277–84.

34. Cf. discussion of "the prophets of peace" in Franklin H. Littell, "Concern for the Human Person," in *Primacy of the Person in the Church* (Notre Dame, Ind.: Fides Publishers, 1967), pp. 54–56.

35. Gordis, "A Cruel God or None—Is There No Other Choice?" p. 277.

36. Sup., p. 60.

37. Richard Kerwohl, "Politisches Messiastum," *Zwischen den Zeiten* 11 (1931): 19–43.

38. Quoted in Fritz Stern, *The Politics of Cultural Despair* (Los Angeles: University of California Press, 1963), p. 259. Emphasizing the Nazi flight from present history, the author comments: "Its followers sought to destroy the despised present in order to recapture an ideological past in an imaginary future" (p. xvi).

39. Cf. article "Primitivismus" in *Weltkirchenlexikon: Handbuch der Oekumene,* ed. Franklin H. Littell and Hans Hermann Walz (Stuttgart: Kreuz Verlag, 1960), cols. 1182–87.

40. For extensive discussion of this point see Koppel S. Pinson, "Pietism, A Source of German Nationalism," 1 *Christendom* (1936) 2:267; also his *Pietism as a Factor in the Rise of German Nationalism* (New York: Columbia University Press, 1934).

41. Duncan Howlett, *The Fourth Faith* (New York: Harper & Row, 1964), pp. 58, 214.

42. Eugen Rosenstock-Huessy, "Das Volk Gottes in Vergangenheit, Gegenwart, Zukunft," in *Juden/ Christen/ Deutsche,* p. 200.

43. Arthur C. Cochrane, *The Church's Confession Under Hitler* (Philadelphia: Westminster Press, 1962), p. 57.

44. Robert Welch, *The Blue Book of the John Birch Society* (n.p.: privately printed, 1961), 11th printing, pp. 63, 147, 150.

45. According to a general survey, over 80 percent of Americans believed the Bible to be the revealed word of God, but 53 percent could not give the name of one of the first four books of the New Testament! Will Herberg, *Protestant-Catholic-Jew* (Garden City, N.Y.: Doubleday & Co., 1955), p. 14.

46. Avraham Shapira, et al., *The Seventh Day,* p. 23.

47. Elie Wiesel, *The Town Beyond the Wall* (New York: Avon Books, 1969), p. 84.

48. Note 1: Our high-school and small-college authorities might improve their educational programs, and especially their school governance, very considerably if they could remember that they are dealing now with young adults and not "children." Note 2: A substantial dimension of totalitarian atavism is "the politics of adolescence," in which through parades and chants and dances and political revivals the demagogues of the party carry the crowd back to the uncomplex monism of preadult life.

49. Cf. Elie Wiesel, *Souls on Fire* (New York: Random House, 1972).

50. Robert L. Lindsey, *An Introduction to the Theology of the Jewish Christian Relationship* (Jerusalem: Dugith Publishers, 1969), p. 12.

51. Emil L. Fackenheim, "The People Israel Lives," 87 *Christian Century* (1970) 18:568; see also Alice L. Eckardt, "Christian and Jewish Responses to the Holocaust," a paper delivered at the Annual Meeting of the American Academy of Religion, Chicago, Nov. 8–11, 1973.

APPENDIX A

A Statement to our Fellow Christians*

1. The Church of Christ is rooted in the life of the People Israel. We Christians look upon Abraham as our spiritual ancestor and father of our faith. For us the relationship is not one of physical descent but the inheritance of a faith like that of Abraham whose life was based on his trust in the promises made to him by God (Gen. 15:1–6). The ministry of Jesus and the life of the early Christian community were thoroughly rooted in the Judaism of their day, particularly in the teachings of the Pharisees. The Christian Church is still sustained by the living faith of the patriarchs and prophets, kings and priests, scribes and rabbis, and the people whom God chose for his own. Christ is the link (Gal. 3: 26–29) enabling the Gentiles to be numbered among Abraham's "off-spring" and therefore fellowheirs with the Jews according to God's promise. It is a tragedy of history that Jesus, our bond of unity with the Jews, has all too often become a symbol and source of division and bitterness because of human weakness and pride.

---

*This statement was released in the summer of 1973 by a group of Christian theologians who worked for four years on the subject "Israel: the People, the Land, the State." The group was convened and assisted by the Commission on Faith and Order of the National Council of Churches of Christ in collaboration with the Secretariat for Catholic-Jewish Relations of the National Conference of Catholic Bishops. The group studied and discussed papers by Jewish and Muslim scholars, as well as by Christians. The secretary of the Theological Working Party has been from the beginning Sister Ann Patrick Ware. The chairman for the first three years was Professor Littell; he was succeeded in October 1972 by Professor Pawlikowski. Study papers on various aspects of the group's work are available.

134

2. Christians can also enrich themselves by a careful study of postbiblical Judaism to the present day. Such enrichment is especially imperative in light of the far-reaching value crisis that now affects the entire Western world. If religion is to play its rightful role in the value reconstruction that is now beginning, its approach will have to be ecumenical. And in the West this means, first of all, the recognition that two religious traditions, not a single Judaeo-Christian tradition, have shaped our culture; and secondly, the genuine and open sharing of insights and differences between Jews and Christians, each realizing that one's understanding of the spiritual nature of the human person remains incomplete without the other.

3. The singular grace of Jesus Christ does not abrogate the covenantal relationship of God with Israel (Rom. 11:1-2). In Christ the Church shares in Israel's election without superseding it. By baptism and faith the Christian, as the Roman liturgy says, passes over to the sonship of Abraham and shares in the dignity of Israel. The survival of the Jewish people, despite the barbaric persecutions and the cruel circumstances under which they were forced to live, is a sign of God's continuing fidelity to the people dear to him. For our spiritual legacy and for all that the Jews have done for the whole human race we Christians are grateful to God and to the people whom God has chosen as a special instrument of his kindness.

4. The new ecumenical atmosphere in theological research and the tragic reality of the Holocaust together with the present Middle East conflict urge us to reconsider the relationship of Christians to Jews. We Christians have readily acknowledged that God made a covenant with the Jews in the past, promising his paternal care for his chosen people in return for their fidelity. Unfortunately many Christians have assumed that the validity of Judaism ended with the beginning of Christianity, the rejection of Jesus as Messiah marking the dissolution of the covenant. This assumption conflicts sharply with Paul's declaration that God did not annul his promise to the chosen people since God never takes back his gifts or revokes his call (Rom. 11:28-29). The Apostle dismissed as altogether untenable the notion that God had rejected his people. There is thus strong Scriptural support for the position that God's covenant love for the Jewish people remains firm. The continuity of contemporary Judaism with ancient Israel demonstrates the abiding validity of Jewish worship and life as authentic forms of service to the true God.

5. The fierce persecution of Jews by Christians through the centuries should be seen as a fratricidal strife as well as a vast human tragedy. In many instances Christian preachers and writers disseminated slanderous stories about the Jews. From the apostolic age the Church accepted uncritically the condemnation of the Pharisees as hypocrites even though the Synoptic Gospels picture Jesus as generally agreeing with what many Pharisees in fact stood for. Whole generations of Christians looked with contempt upon this people who were condemned to remain wanderers on the earth on the charge, in fact false, of having killed Christ. Anti-Jewish polemics became a perennial feature of Christendom and reflected gross ignorance of Jewish history and religion. This sin has infected the non-Christian world as well.

6. A major source of friction in contemporary Christian-Jewish relations is Christian hostility and indifference to the State of Israel. In dialogue among Christians on the Middle East question there exists a startling variety of opinions, some of which exacerbate already existing Christian-Jewish misunderstandings. We urge the churches therefore to give their prayerful attention to such central questions as the legitimacy of the Jewish state, the rights of the Palestinians, and the problem of the refugees—Jewish as well as Arab. Only a conscience seeking to be well-informed and free of prejudice can help to bring about peace with justice in the Middle East.

7. The validity of the State of Israel rests on moral and juridical grounds. It was established in response to a resolution of the U.N. General Assembly, after termination of the British Mandate. However, involved in the potentially explosive political conflict in the Middle East is a theological question that demands careful scrutiny. What is the relationship between "the people" and "the land"? What is the relation between the chosen people and the territory comprising the present State of Israel? There is no Christian consensus on these questions. Genesis explicitly affirms a connection between the people and the land (Gen. 15:18), and even within the New Testament certain passages imply such a connection. Therefore, Christians who see Israel as something more than a political state are not wrongly theologizing politics by understanding the existence of the Jewish state in theological terms. They are merely recognizing that modern Israel is the homeland of a people whose political identity is sustained by the faith that God has blessed them with a covenant. There is reason for Chris-

tians to rejoice that the Jewish people are no longer required to live in enforced dispersion among the nations, separated from the land of promise.

8. We have traditionally viewed the Jews as a people having a universal dimension. God wanted them to set up a special society dedicated to the fulfillment of the messianic aspirations for righteousness and freedom. Even when dispersed they became a summons to the human conscience to safeguard and protect the rights of all people. Here in the United States the Jewish contribution to the advancement of human rights remains outstanding. Now the question arises: Is the Jewish people so universalistic as to exclude the possibility of their having a state of their own? It does seem to many observers that the localizing of Jewish activities gives a greater opportunity to fulfill their universal vocation than would an unfocused global presence.

9. As a political state, Israel is open to all the temptations of power. The charge is sometimes made that Israel is belligerently expansionistic as a result of its military triumphs in the Six-Day War. Visitors to Israel, however, can easily discover that the overriding concern of the majority of Israelis is peace, not more territory. Israel's anxiety about national defense reflects the age-old human yearning for security, the anxiety of a people whose history has been a saga of frightful persecution, climaxed by the Holocaust of six million men, women and children. Against such a tormented background, is it surprising that the Jewish people should want to defend themselves? It would be quite unrealistic and unjust to expect Israel to become a sort of heavenly society of which more is expected than of other nations. This does not mean that Christians must endorse every policy decision by the Israeli government. Most Jews, both within Israel and without, do not do so. Rather, Christians must refrain from the type of criticism that would use the failure of Israel to live up to the highest moral standards as an excuse to deny its right to exist. Such a view would be a double standard, one not applied to any other nation on earth.

10. As Christians we urge all nations in the world (our own nation, Israel, and the Arab states included) to recognize that there is no way to secure lasting peace based on the balance of military power and the use of fear as a deterrent. Rather, the only road leading to peace is trust in and understanding of neighbors and partners. We urge the Church to attend to its role as agent of reconciliation.

11. At present antisemitism is unfashionable and seems to have gone underground in the United States, though some recent studies show it is on the rise. But even an underground antisemitism surfaces from time to time in various forms and disguises. New Left literature has excoriated the Jews not as Jews but as Zionists. Some Christian publications in the United States and Canada have even resorted to more subtle forms of antisemitism, exploiting the claim that Israel is "judaizing" Jerusalem and its environs and driving Arabs from their homes in the Holy City. Antisemitism, however, is a difficult virus to counteract. It has a pervasiveness that infects our whole civilization and manifests itself in education, housing, job opportunities and social life. Fortunately some Christian churches are working hard to excise from their liturgy and education any antisemitic references.

12. Those who refuse to learn from history must relive the errors and evils of the past. In times of civil disorders, agitators have arisen and will continue to appear in our society attempting to make the Jews the scapegoats for the evils of an era. If problems like inflation and unemployment continue to escalate, if a depression should set in, we can be fairly sure that the radical Right and/or the radical Left will make Jews out to be the culprits.

13. The pressure of our violent times urges us as Christians to live up to our calling as ministers of reconciliation, ready and willing to stifle rumors about the Jews and to build up an atmosphere of brotherly understanding in Christian-Jewish relations. We strongly commend Jewish-Christian dialogue as a favored instrument by which we may explore the richness of Judaism and the Jewish roots of our Christian faith.

14. The pain of the past has taught us that antisemitism is a Pandora's box from which spring not only atrocities against Jews but also contempt for Christ. Whatever the antisemite inflicts on the Jews he inflicts on Christ who is "bone of their bone and flesh of their flesh." In the words of St. Paul, "They are Israelites and to them belong the sonship, the glory, the covenants, the giving of law, the worship and the promises; to them belong the patriarchs, and of their race according to the flesh is the Christ" (Rom. 9:4–5).

Signers of the statement, who were also members of the study group (with church and institutional affiliations given for identification):

Dr. Markus Barth
University of Basel
Basel, Switzerland
(Reformed Church, formerly
United Presbyterian)

Dr. Roland de Corneille
National Director, League
for Human Rights
Toronto, Canada
(Anglican)

Dr. A. Roy Eckardt
Lehigh University
Bethlehem, Pennsylvania
(United Methodist)

The Rev. Edward H. Flannery
Secretariat for Catholic-Jewish
Relations
Washington, D.C.
(Roman Catholic)

Dr. Robert T. Handy
Union Theological Seminary
New York City
(American Baptist)

Dr. Walter J. Harrelson, Dean
Vanderbilt Divinity School
Nashville, Tennessee
(American Baptist/Disciples of
Christ)

The Rev. William H. Harter
Margaretville-New Kingston
Parish
Margaretville, New York
(United Presbyterian)

Dr. Franklin H. Littell
Temple University
Philadelphia, Pennsylvania
(United Methodist)

Msgr. John M. Oesterreicher,
Director
Institute of Judaeo-Christian
Studies
Seton Hall University
South Orange, New Jersey
(Roman Catholic)

Dr. Bernhard E. Olson
National Director of
Interreligious Affairs
National Conference of
Christians and Jews
New York City
(United Methodist)

The Rev. John T. Pawlikowski,
O.M.I.
Catholic Theological Union
Chicago, Illinois
(Roman Catholic)

Rt. Rev. Leo Rudloff, O.S.B.,
Abbot
Benedictine Priory
Weston, Vermont
(Roman Catholic)

Dr. J. Coert Rylaarsdam
Marquette University
Milwaukee, Wisconsin
(Reformed Church in America)

The Rev. John B. Sheerin, C.S.P.
The New Catholic World
New York City
(Roman Catholic)

The Rev. Theodore
Stylianopoulos
Holy Cross Greek Orthodox
Seminary
Brookline, Massachusetts
(Greek Orthodox)

Sister Rose Thering, O.P.
Institute of Judaeo-Christian
    Studies
Seton Hall University
South Orange, New Jersey
(Roman Catholic)

Dr. John T. Townsend
Philadelphia Divinity School
Philadelphia, Pennsylvania
(Episcopal)

Dr. Hans Eberhard von Waldow
Pittsburgh Theological Seminary
Pittsburgh, Pennsylvania
(Lutheran Church in America)

APPENDIX B

A Yom HaShoah Liturgy for Christians

In ancient sacred ritual a holocaust was the most costly of animal sacrifices: an offering in which the victim was totally consumed by fire. In the mid-twentieth century the word has acquired a new force: "the Holocaust" means the destruction of European Jewry by the Nazis, 1933–1945.*

Voices of the Holocaust

1. **To reach into the darkness.**

A whirlwind cannot be taught; it must be experienced. And we cannot know what happened during the *Shoah*—that whirlwind of destruction in which Hitler's Germany killed six million Jews—solely by learning historical facts and figures and scholarly explanations. Facts, figures, and explanations are necessary. But we must also touch

---

*This program was planned by Dr. Elizabeth Wright and conducted in the Chapel at Queens College, Charlotte, N.C., on May 10, 1972. She spoke the transitional parts, read several of the selections, and led the closing prayer. The other selections were read by students who had been members of a course entitled "The Star and the Swastika: a Study of Jewish Holocaust Literature" during the January term, 1972. The service lasted about thirty-five minutes. The service was reprinted by Christians Concerned for Israel and is used by a growing number of Christian groups. The date of Yom HaShoah is fixed in the Jewish calendar, which means that it changes each year in the calendar commonly used. In 1975 the observation is April 8. Christian readers will find help in fixing the date for other years and in locating resource books from a local rabbi.

and feel and taste the dark days and the burning nights. Our hearts must constrict in terror and grief. Our minds must expand to make room for the incredible. And our love for the goodness of life must grow strong enough to reach into the darkness and to discover the heart of that darkness, the experience itself.

Darkness pervaded every street of every town, city, and country occupied by Nazi Germany. The innermost circle of this geography of hell was the concentration camp. Once inside this circle, humanity moved from the light of day to the valley of the shadow of death. Yet, life did go on. And the testimony of survivors of that life reaches out to us, demanding our concern, our attention, our anguish, and our dedication for tasks left undone, for an expansion of our own existence which must come to encompass those six million lives and bring them back into a world which must not and dares not forget all that took place.

And so we must enter the past. But what passport will gain us entry into hell? Recognizing the fact that the world we are about to enter is utterly alien to the world we know, how can we expand the horizons of our awareness so that hell and the experience of it become real? Two paths are open to us: we can add to our knowledge of the past and strive to understand the outer structure and details of the police state achieved by Hitler Germany. And we can add to our knowledge of ourselves, of man's inner nature—of that range of emotions moving from love to hate and fear of death—only as we experience the daily lives of those who lived within the hell that was Nazi Germany. Facts are of little use in this second quest. But in the literature of that period it is not only facts but emotions which are transmitted. And the knowledge of the evil which can reside in us is too heavy a burden for reason or intellect to carry. Somehow, we must enter the Holocaust and its geography in this twofold way: with a clear mind, and with the humility and openness linked in the Bible with the contrite soul. Only then will we see, and seeing, understand.

Albert H. Friedlander, ed, *Out of the Whirlwind: A Reader of Holocaust Literature* (New York: Union of American Hebrew Congregations and Doubleday & Co., 1968), pp. 11–12.

2. Why do I write?

Some voices of the Holocaust are words written urgently by those who perished soon after in the ghettos or the death camps. Chaim Kaplan kept a secret diary in the Warsaw Ghetto:

The terrible events have engulfed me; the horrible deeds committed in the ghetto have so frightened and stunned me that I have not the power, either physical or spiritual, to review these events and perpetuate them with the pen of a scribe. I have no words to express what has happened to us since the day the expulsion was ordered. Those people who have gotten some notion of historical expulsions from books know nothing. We, the inhabitants of the Warsaw Ghetto, are now experiencing the reality. Our only good fortune is that our days are numbered—that we shall not have long to live under conditions like these, and that after our terrible sufferings and wanderings we shall come to eternal rest, which was denied us in life. Among ourselves we fully admit that this death which lurks behind our walls will be our salvation; but there is one thorn. We shall not be privileged to witness the downfall of the Nazis, which in the end will surely come to pass.

Some of my friends and acquaintances who know the secret of my diary urge me, in their despair, to stop writing. "Why? For what purpose? Will you live to see it published? Will these words of yours reach the ears of future generations? How? If you are deported you won't be able to take it with you because the Nazis will watch your every move, and even if you succeed in hiding it when you leave Warsaw, you will undoubtedly die on the way, for your strength is ebbing. And if you don't die from lack of strength, you will die by the Nazi sword. For not a single deportee will be able to hold out to the end of the war."

And yet in spite of it all I refuse to listen to them. I feel that continuing this diary to the very end of my physical and spiritual strength is a historical mission which must not be abandoned. My mind is still clear, my need to record unstilled, though it is now five days since any real food has passed my lips. Therefore I will not silence my diary! (July 26, 1942.)

Chaim A. Kaplan, *Scroll of Agony,* in Freidlander, ed., *Out of the Whirlwind,* p. 189. From *Scroll of Agony,* ed. and trans. Abraham I. Katsh (New York: Macmillan, 1965).

3. The voice of a child in the Terezin camp.

"The Butterfly," a poem written in camp by Paul Friedman, age 11:

> The last, the very last
> So richly, brightly, dazzlingly yellow.

Perhaps if the sun's tears would sing
against a white stone . . .

Such, such a yellow
Is carried lightly 'way up high
It went away I'm sure because it wished to kiss the world goodbye.

For seven weeks I've lived in here,
Penned up inside this ghetto
But I have found my people here.
The dandelions call to me
And the white chestnut candles in the court,
Only I never saw another butterfly.

That butterfly was the last one.
Butterflies don't live in here,
In the ghetto.

Hana Volavkova, ed., *I Never Saw Another Butterfly* (New York: McGraw-Hill Book Co., 1964). Used with permission of the publisher.

4. Our bodies beginning to devour themselves; one literally became a number.

Others, who survived the Nazi years, speak to us of their experience as prisoners. Viktor Frankl, a doctor:

When the last layers of subcutaneous fat had vanished, and we looked like skeletons disguised with skin and rags, we could watch our bodies beginning to devour themselves. The organism digested its own protein, and the muscles disappeared. Then the body had no powers of resistance left. One after another the members of the little community in our hut died. Each of us could calculate with fair accuracy whose turn would be next, and when his own would come. After many observations we knew the symptoms well, which made the correctness of our prognoses quite certain. "He won't last long," or, "This is the next one," we whispered to each other, and when, during our daily search for lice, we saw our own naked bodies in the evening, we thought alike: This body here, my body, is really a corpse already. What has become of me? I am but a small portion of a great mass of human flesh . . . of a mass behind barbed wire, crowded into a few earthen huts; a mass of which daily a certain portion begins to rot because it has become lifeless.

It is very difficult for an outsider to grasp how very little value was placed on human life in camp. The camp inmate was hardened, but possibly became more conscious of this complete disregard of human existence when a convoy of sick men was arranged. The emaciated bodies of the sick were thrown on two-wheeled carts which were drawn by prisoners for many miles, often through snowstorms, to the next camp. If one of the sick men had died before the cart left, he was thrown on anyway—the list had to be correct! The list was the only thing that mattered. A man counted only because he had a prison number. One literally became a number: dead or alive—that was unimportant; the life of a "number" was completely irrelevant. What stood behind that number and that life mattered even less: the fate, the history, the name of the man.

> Viktor Frankl, *Man's Search for Meaning* (Boston: Beacon Press, 1963), pp. 47–48, 83.

These voices are vitally important to us, the survivors. For in a sense we are all survivors. What our generation has to live with—not just Jews, but all of us—is the fact that the Nazi holocaust brought an end to a certain kind of innocence. In the light of what happened, we know now that there is practically no limit to the horror which men are capable of perpetrating and that only we ourselves can stand in the way to prevent its happening again.

5. Terrifying torment of the spirit.

The physical agony suffered during the holocaust was appalling. But these voices tell us also of a truly terrifying torment of the spirit, dominated by the victims' feeling of complete isolation from the rest of the world. And beyond this human silence lay the even more terrifying silence of God.

In any case, by one road or another, they almost all reached the "Heart of Darkness"; fell victims to the "Final Solution." The physical agony suffered requires no further comment. But what comes through in all the books written on the subject is the truly terrifying torment of the spirit—the feeling of complete isolation from the rest of the world—the feeling (amply justified) that in their hour of agony they were abandoned by nearly all of mankind. We are concerned here not with the moral implications of this failure of mankind (though there were notable exceptions, such as the case of the Danes who saw to it that almost no Jews fell into Nazi hands); we are concerned, rather, with the impact this failure had on the spirit of the camp inmates. The eyes and ears of humanity seemed shut, and not a move, not even a token gesture was forthcoming to bring, if not help, at least a message of hope.

> Ernst Pawel, film lecture, "Writings of the Nazi Holocaust," available from the Audio-Visual Department, Anti-Defamation League, 315 Lexington Avenue, New York, N.Y. 10016; pamphlet pp. 10–11.

6. Never shall I forget that night.

Elie Wiesel was 14 years old, a village boy, sheltered and deeply religious, when he was taken in a convoy to Auschwitz. He writes of that midnight when they reached the camp:

Never shall I forget that night, the first night in camp, which has turned my life into one long night, seven times cursed and seven times sealed. Never shall I forget that smoke. Never shall I forget the little faces of the children, whose bodies I saw turned to wreaths of smoke beneath a silent blue sky.

Never shall I forget those flames which consumed my faith forever.

Never shall I forget that nocturnal silence which deprived me, for all eternity, of the desire to live. Never shall I forget those moments which murdered my God and my soul and turned my dreams to dust. Never shall I forget these things, even if I am condemned to live as long as God Himself. Never.

> Elie Wiesel, *Night* (New York: Hill & Wang, 1969), p. 44.

7. One day, when we came back from work, we saw three gallows.

Again Elie Wiesel, describing an execution ceremony in the concentration camp:

One day, when we came back from work, we saw three gallows rearing up in the assembly place, three black crows. Roll call. SS all around us, machine guns trained: the traditional ceremony. Three victims in chains—and one of them, the little servant, the sad-eyed angel.

The SS seemed more preoccupied, more disturbed than usual. To hang a young boy in front of thousands of spectators was no light matter. The head of the camp read the verdict. All eyes were on the child. He was lividly pale, almost calm, biting his lips. The gallows threw its shadow over him.

This time the Lagerkapo refused to act as executioner. Three SS replaced him.

The three victims mounted together onto the chairs.

The three necks were placed at the same moment within the nooses.

"Long live liberty!" cried the two adults.

But the child was silent.

"Where is God? Where is He?" someone behind me asked.

At a sign from the head of the camp, the three chairs tipped over.

Total silence throughout the camp. On the horizon, the sun was setting.

"Bare your heads!" yelled the head of the camp. His voice was raucous. We were weeping.

"Cover your heads!"

Then the march past began. The two adults were no longer alive. Their tongues hung swollen, blue-tinged. But the third rope was still moving; being so light, the child was still alive. . . .

For more than half an hour he stayed there, struggling between life and death, dying in slow agony under our eyes. And we had to look him full in the face. He was still alive when I passed in front of him. His tongue was still red, his eyes were not yet glazed.

Behind me, I heard the same man asking:

"Where is God now?"

And I heard a voice within me answer him:

"Where is He? Here He is—He is hanging here on this gallows. . . ."

That night the soup tasted of corpses.

Night, pp. 75–76.

8. O the Chimneys

The spiritual night of the concentration camps destroyed not only the intended victims but the executioners themselves, those clever technicians of death. The poet Nelly Sachs invokes the smoking chimneys of the crematories:

> O the chimneys
> On the ingeniously devised habitations of death
> When Israel's body drifted as smoke
> Through the air—
> Was welcomed by a star, a chimney sweep,
> A star that turned black
> Or was it a ray of sun?
>
> O the chimneys!
> Freedomway for Jeremiah and Job's dust—

Who devised you and laid stone upon stone
The road for refugees of smoke?

O the habitations of death,
Invitingly appointed
For the host who used to be a guest—
O you fingers
Laying the threshold
Like a knife between life and death—

O you chimneys,
O you fingers
And Israel's body as smoke through the air!

Nelly Sachs, *O the Chimneys,* trans. Michael Hamburger (New York: Farrar, Straus & Giroux, 1967), p. 3. Copyright © 1967 by Farrar, Straus and Giroux, Inc. Reprinted with the permission of Farrar, Straus and Giroux, Inc.

9. On Jewish Resistance

At the time of Hitler and ever since, Jews have energetically debated the question of their resistance against the Nazis: whether to resist, why, how, to what avail. One view in this continuing debate is that of Alexander Donat, in his memoirs of the Warsaw Ghetto:

There was a stubborn, unending, continuous battle to survive. In view of the unequal forces, it was a labor of Sisyphus. Jewish resistance was the resistance of a fish caught in a net, a mouse in a trap, an animal at bay. It is pure myth that the Jews were merely "passive," that they did not resist the Nazis who had decided on their destruction. The Jews fought back against their enemies to a degree no other community anywhere in the world would have been capable of doing were it to find itself similarly beleaguered. They fought against hunger and starvation, against epidemic disease, against the deadly Nazi economic blockade. They fought against the German murderers and against the traitors within their own ranks, *and they were utterly alone in their fight.* They were forsaken by God and man, surrounded by the hatred or indifference of the Gentile population.

Ours was not a romantic war. Although there was much heroism, there was little beauty; much toil and suffering, but no glamor. We fought back on every front where the enemy attacked—the biological front, the economic front, the propaganda front, the cultural front—with every weapon we possessed.

In the end it was ruse, deception and cunning beyond anything the world has ever seen, which accomplished what hunger and disease could not achieve. What defeated us, ultimately, was Jewry's indestructible optimism, our eternal faith in the goodness of man—or rather, in the limits of his degradation. For generations, the Jews of Eastern Europe had looked to Berlin as to the very symbol of lawfulness, enlightenment and culture. We just could not believe that a German, even disguised as a Nazi, would so far renounce his own humanity as to murder women and children—coldly and systematically. We paid a terrible price for our hope, which turned out to be a delusion: the delusion that the nation of Kant, Goethe, Mozart and Beethoven cannot be a nation of murderers. And when, finally, we saw how we had been deceived, and we resorted to the weapons for which we were least well prepared—historically, philosophically, psychologically—when we finally took up arms, we inscribed in the annals of history the unforgettable epic of the Warsaw Ghetto uprising.

> Alexander Donat, "The Holocaust Kingdom," in Friedlander, ed., *Out of the Whirlwind*, pp. 57–58. From *Jewish Resistance* (Flint, Mich.: Walden Press, 1964).

10. Why do the Christians hate us?

Among the many and complex factors which made possible the rise of Nazism, there is no doubt that one essential factor was the centuries-long history of Christian hostility, oppression, and sporadic violence against the Jews. Without this potent anti-Jewish poison in the blood-stream of Christian Europe, without the superstitions and religious dogmas which had long been used to justify it, the Nazi program would never have been so hideously successful.

This ancient evil of Christian hostility toward the Jew is the theme of a conversation in Andre Schwarz-Bart's novel The Last of the Just. *Ernie and Golda are two young Jews who meet in Paris during the Nazi occupation.*

"Oh Ernie," Golda said, "you know them. Tell me why, *why* do the Christians hate us the way they do? They seem so nice when I can look at them without my star."

Ernie put his arm around her shoulders solemnly. "It's very mysterious," he murmured in Yiddish. "They don't know exactly why themselves. I've been in their churches and I've read their gospel. Do you know who the Christ was? A simple Jew like your father. A kind of Hasid."

Golda smiled gently. "You're kidding me."

"No, no, believe me, and I'll bet they'd have got along fine the two

of them, because he was really a good Jew you know, sort of like the
Baal Shem Tov—a merciful man, and gentle. The Christians say they
love him, but I think they hate him without knowing it. So they take
the cross by the other end and make a sword out of it and strike us with
it! You understand, Golda," he cried suddenly, strangely excited, *"they
take the cross and they turn it around, they turn it around, my God ..."*
    "Sh, quiet," Golda said. "They'll hear you." And stroking the scars
on Ernie's forehead, as she often liked to do, she smiled. "And you
promised you wouldn't 'think' all afternoon. . . ."
    Ernie kissed the hand that had caressed his forehead and went on
stubbornly, "Poor Jesus, if he came back to earth and saw that the
pagans had made a sword out of him and used it against his sisters and
brothers, he'd be sad, he'd grieve forever. And maybe he does see it.
They say that some of the Just Men remain outside the gates of Para-
dise, that they don't want to forget humanity, that they too await the
Messiah. Yes, maybe he sees it. Who knows? You understand, Goldeleh,
he was a little old-fashioned Jew, a real Just Man, you know, no more
nor less than . . . all our Just Men. And it's true, he and your father
would have got along together. I can see them *so* well together, you
know. 'Now,' your father would say, 'now my good rabbi, doesn't it
break your heart to see all that?' And the other would tug at his beard
and say, 'But you know very well, my good Samuel, that the Jewish
heart must break a thousand times for the greater good of all peoples.
That is why we were chosen, didn't you know?' And your father would
say, 'Oi, oi, didn't I know? Didn't I know? Oh, excellent rabbi, that's
all I *do* know, alas. . . .' "
    They laughed. Golda took her harmonica from the bottom of the
basket, flashed sunlight off it into Ernie's eyes, and still smiling brought
it to her lips and played a forbidden melody. It was Hatikvah, the
ancient chant of hope, and as she inspected the Square Mouton-Duver-
net with uneasy eyes, she tasted the sweetness of forbidden fruit. Ernie
leaned down and plucked a tuft of slightly mildewed grass and planted
the blades in Golda's still moist hair. As they got up to leave he tried
to strip her of that poor garland, but she stopped his hand. "Too bad
about the people who see. And too bad about the Germans too. Today
I say too bad about everybody. Everybody . . ." she repeated, unexpectedly solemn.

Andre Schwarz-Bart, *The Last of the Just*, trans. Stephen Becker (New
York: Atheneum, 1960), pp. 365–367. Copyright © 1960 by Atheneum
House, Inc. Copyright © 1959 by Editions du Seuil, Paris. Reprinted by
permission of Atheneum Publishers, U.S.A., and Martin Secker & War-
burg Ltd.

11. Chorus of the Rescued

Within a few months, both Ernie and Golda were dead in a gas chamber. For those Jews who did not die, but who somehow outlasted the wreckage of the Third Reich, there was the pain of learning to re-enter the world. The poet Nelly Sachs gives them voices in her "Chorus of the Rescued":

We, the rescued,
From whose hollow bones death had begun to whittle his flutes,
And on whose sinews he had already stroked his bow—
Our bodies continue to lament
With their mutilated music.
We, the rescued,
The nooses would for our necks still dangle
before us in the blue air—
Hourglasses still fill with our dripping blood.
We, the rescued,
The worms of fear still feed on us.
Our constellation is buried in dust.
We, the rescued,
Beg you:
Show us your sun, but gradually,
Lead us from star to star, step by step.
Be gentle when you teach us to live again.
Lest the song of a bird,
Or a pail being filled at the well,
Let our badly sealed pain burst forth again
and carry us away—
We beg you:
Do not show us an angry dog, not yet—
It could be, it could be
That we will dissolve into dust—
Dissolve into dust before your eyes.
For what binds our fabric together?
We whose breath vacated us,
Whose soul fled to Him out of that midnight
Long before our bodies were rescued
Into the ark of the moment.
We, the rescued,
We press your hand
We look into your eye—

But all that binds us together now is leave-taking,
The leave-taking in the dust
Binds us together with you.

"Chorus of the Rescued," a choral reading by three, Nelly Sachs, *O the
Chimneys*, trans. Michael Hamburger (New York: Farrar, Straus & Gi-
roux, 1967) pp. 25–27. Copyright © 1967 by Farrar, Straus and Giroux,
Inc. Reprinted with the permission of Farrar, Straus and Giroux, Inc.

12. The Resurrection—An elegy for the six million

*The voices of the dead, the rescued, and the living have become a
growing chorus in our time as Jews take up the task of remembering,
of teaching their children, of bearing witness before the world. Some
congregations now use this poem by David Polish in their liturgy for
the Days of Awe (the solemn period of the Day of Atonement and the
New Year). It is entitled "The Resurrection—An elegy for the six million":*

One day they will assemble in the valley of bones—
Ashes sifted out of furnaces, vapors from Luneburg,
Parchments from some friend's books, cakes of soap,
Half-formed embryos, screams still heard in nightmares.
God will breathe upon them. He will say: Be men.

> *But they will defy Him: We do not hear you. Did you hear us?*
> *There is no resurrection for us. In life it was a wondrous thing*
> *For each of us to be himself, to guide his limbs to do his will.*
> *But the many are now one. Our blood has flowed together,*
> *Our ashes are inseparable, our marrow commingled,*
> *Our voices poured together like water of the sea.*
> *We shall not surrender this greater self.*
> *We the Abrahams, Isaacs, Jacobs, Sarahs, Leahs, Rachels*
> *Are now forever Israel.*

Almighty God, raise up a man who will go peddling through the world.
Let him gather us up and go through the world selling us as trinkets.
Let the peddler sell us cheaply. Let him hawk his wares and say:
Who will buy my souvenirs? Little children done in soap,
A rare Germanic parchment of the greatest Jew in Lodz.
Men will buy us and display us and point to us with pride:
A thousand Jews went into this and here is a rare piece
That came all the way from Crakow in a box car.
A great statesman will place a candle at his bedside.
It will burn but never be consumed.

The tallow will drip with the tears we shed.
And it will glow with the souls of our children.
They will put us in the bathrooms of the United Nations
Where diplomats will wash and wash their hands
With Polish Jews and German Jews and Russian Jews.
Let the peddler sell the box of soap that was once buried
With Kaddish and Psalms by our brothers.

> *Some night the statesman will blow upon the candle*
> *And it will not go out.*
> *The souls of little children will flicker and flicker*
> *But not expire.*
> *Some day the diplomats will wash their hands and find*
>   *them stained with blood.*
> *Some day the citizens of the German town*
> *Will awake to find their houses reeking*
> *With all the vapors from all the concentration camps,*
> *From Hell itself, and the stench will come from the*
> *Soap box.*

Then they will all rise up, statesmen, diplomats, citizens
And go hunting for the peddler: You who disturb our rest
And our ablutions, you who haunt us with your souvenirs,
You who prick our conscience, death upon you!

> *But the peddlers shall never cease from the earth*
> *Until the candles die out and the soap melts away.*

David Polish, in *High Holy Day Prayerbook*, ed. Mordecai M. Kaplan, Eugene Kohn, and Ira Eisenstein (New York: Jewish Reconstructionist Foundation, 1948), Vol II, pp. 404–405.

LET US PRAY. *God of Israel, our God, God of all humanity, help us to learn how to listen to such messengers. We have so little bravery of mind, so little of the humble and contrite heart, which would enable us to heed their words. In many and various ways you spoke of old to our fathers by the prophets and through Jesus the Jew, our fellow man whom we allege to be your Son. Help us to hear the voices which you send today. Strengthen now our trust in the goodness of life, strengthen us for tasks yet to be done, so that no earthly darkness may be able to overwhelm us.*

AMEN.

SHALOM ALEICHEM!